God bless

The Principle Centered Life

Paradox -- or Positive Living?

Wil Watson

authorHOUSE®

AuthorHouse™
1663 Liberty Drive, Suite 200
Bloomington, IN 47403
www.authorhouse.com
Phone: 1-800-839-8640

First published by AuthorHouse   11/13/2008

ISBN: 978-1-4389-1060-4 (sc)
ISBN: 978-1-4389-1059-8 (hc)

Library of Congress Control Number: 2008907555

Printed in the United States of America
Bloomington, Indiana

This book is printed on acid-free paper.

Table of Contents

PREFACE

Decisions. Options. Choices. Alternatives. We face them every day. So, how do we decide what to do? Flip a coin? Roll the dice? Take a public opinion poll? Use our powers of reason? Ask God for guidance? Or, is something more needed?

How about some settled life principles to guide us? Living without them is like traveling to an unfamiliar destination without a roadmap. It's like hiking in a dense forest without a compass. There's no clear sense of direction. There's no magnetic north to give order and aim on life's journey. Obviously, God's leadership is crucial. Yet, He has given us the privilege and responsibility of making our own decisions. We're free to choose. And we need a central authority for our choices. In other words, we need to live principle centered lives. When those principles are based on God's Word, we're better equipped to distinguish His specific guidance from the influence of the world around us. Even if they seem paradoxical!

The goal of every sincere Christian is to live a Christ-centered life. He's our pattern. He not only taught the principle centered life, He lived it – when He was tempted to turn stones into bread for His empty stomach; when the cheering crowd wanted to make Him king; when He was mockingly urged to come down from Calvary's cross and avoid death. At the beginning of His ministry, He served notice on Satan that He was living by principle, not personal comfort. When tempted in the wilderness, He countered Satan's enticements three times with "It is written". (See Matthew 4; Luke 4) That's principle-centered living. Want a Christ-centered life? Follow His example!

Life principles do more than guide us in the right direction. They also serve as an anchor when we experience life's storms and the shifting winds of pop culture. They prevent moral relativism and situation ethics. They bring consistency to our actions and focus to our life goals. That's why we need this moral compass.

Obviously, the thirteen chapters of this book do not exhaust the list of important truths to live by. These are simply the ones I chose to present for your consideration. I have found them to be meaningful in my own life. Your list would be different from mine. The focus of this book is on some principles, which, on the surface, seem self-contradictory. Therefore, I refer to them as "paradoxical". Yet, they are both sound and logical. It is my hope that you will find them helpful in your spiritual journey.

While these principles apply to both saint and sinner, their deepest significance is for those committed to loving and serving God. Each has a Biblical and spiritual foundation. The thirteen chapter format is designed to make the book useful for small groups, as well as for individual readers.

In this time of state-sponsored gambling, the term "life's lottery" is sometimes heard. It suggests life itself is simply a gamble. But it's not just the luck of the draw or the roll of the dice. We are not helpless pawns on a cosmic chessboard. We are not powerless against forces of either Intelligent or unintelligent design. We're not programmed robots. Our Creator has endowed us with rational thought and freedom of choice. So we have the power to make our lives better or worse than our circumstances. That's why positive principles are so important.

May God bless you as you consider these "paradoxical principles". It's my prayer that they will help you experience The Principle Centered Life.

CHAPTER 1

YOU HAVE TO DIE TO REALLY LIVE

There's an old story about a Texas oil tycoon. It seems he left instructions that, upon his death, he was to be buried in his Cadillac automobile. As the car, with his body inside, was being lowered into the oversize grave, an awestruck cemetery worker exclaimed, "Man, that's really livin'!"

We're amused by that quaint story. We picture the scene. We know what the gravedigger meant; he didn't believe the man was really alive. But, wait a minute. Maybe the man was "really livin'" --- if he had gone to heaven. That's the obvious application of our principle: "you have to die to really live". Death can mean eternal life. Since this is a religious book, we'll discuss that important truth. Later. For now, let's see how it applies to life on earth. Everyone lives by principles that determine actions. They may be good or bad. Some lead to a highway of happiness; others point only to dead-end trails. We choose what principles will guide us. And those choices determine our destiny.

Dead-end Life Principles

Our world has many wrong ideas about "real living". In the words of Proverbs 14:12, "There is a way that seems right to a man, but in the end it leads to death." Too many literally are following dead-end paths. Consider these:

"Life in the fast lane" -- We talk longingly of the good old days when life was so much simpler and slower paced. Yet we keep on today's hectic pace. For example, we jump start our children with all kinds of organized activities – then wonder why they grow up too fast. Perhaps it's because we don't allow them to be children long enough.

A recent study found 30% of high school students are drinking caffeine and high energy drinks to keep up the pace. We're all affected by the fast pace of modern life. We can't escape it. But it becomes tragic when it takes control of us. The insidious nature of fast-lane life becomes apparent in our youth, and it continues its strangle-hold on adults. The age at which young people become involved in destructive behavior keeps getting younger. Drugs, alcohol, and promiscuous sex mortgage the future of so many. In 2005, 36.8% of our nation's births were to unwed mothers. (Source: Center for Disease Control and Prevention) Even those who live moral lives are under incredible pressure.

We adults joke "the hurrier I go, the behinder I get." Some of us even take pride in our busy-ness. Speed promises productivity but often delivers "destructivity". Business drive-thrus are everywhere; restaurants, banks, pharmacies, and dry cleaners are among those which cater to life on the run. Internet phone dial-up is now too slow; we must have a high-speed connection. Road rage has become common as drivers react to highway delays. Years ago, Ken Fearing made a colorful description of someone speeding through life: "And wow he lived and wow he died, going wop to the office, and blooey home to sleep, and biff got married and bam had children, and oof got fired. Zowie did he live and zowie did he die." Sounds like a dead end! And it's descriptive of far too many. Maybe they need to experience the "green pastures and quiet waters" David wrote about in Psalm 23.

"Eat, drink and be merry for tomorrow you die" – A more recent version of this hedonistic advice urges "if it feels good, do it". But the consequences may be tragic. Several years ago, a Rubes cartoon, by Leigh Rubin, pictured two goldfish in a bowl. One fish says to the other: "I'm tired of just watching the world go by! I'm going to go out there and experience Life!" The second frame shows the poor little fish lying on the table outside the bowl – dying. That's a powerful commentary on this dead-end principle.

The popular attitude is "it's my body; I can do with it whatever I please." That's true. But there are consequences to living by sensual passions. Galatians 6:7-8 (Living Bible) declares: ". . . a man will always reap just the kind of crop he sows! If he sows to please his own wrong desires. . . he will surely reap a harvest of spiritual decay and death." Once I heard someone joke about his hedonistic lifestyle. He bragged, "I'm gonna be a devil until I become an angel." That's the game plan of far too many. But life doesn't work that way. We don't magically become angels after a lifetime of acting like devils. God isn't anti-pleasure. He wants us to enjoy life. But it's still true that "the wages of sin is death. . ." (Romans 6:23)

He who dies with the most toys wins. --That's not a comforting slogan for dying children. And it's more than an odd bumper sticker. It's an expression of adult obsession with material things. It's about the human desire to accumulate playthings, gadgets, and entertainment devices. Everything from palm-held electronic inventions to fast cars and big boats. Children aren't the only ones who crave toys. One recent Christmas season, customers camped out all night at stores to buy new versions of Play Station and Nintendo at $500 – 600. There were even stampedes, robberies, and shootings as grown-up men grabbed for the newest playthings on the market.

I'm afraid I write this with a bit of smugness. You wouldn't catch me camping out all night so I could buy a Nintendo. No, sir! I'm not obsessed with such "things". But maybe there's something else that rates too high on my scale of values. An innocent "adult toy." Not even very expensive. Hmm! I'll have to think about that. And how about you? What's in your toy chest? The issue isn't, do we own possessions; rather, do our possessions own us? Remember: the best things in life aren't things.

It's a fact: we can't take our "stuff" with us when we die. That's the reason moving vans are not seen in funeral processions. The "toy slogan" admits the fact that, whether we win or lose in life's toy collection, we're going to die. So this is just another dead-end path.

"Physical Fitness can add years to your life." – Yes, it can. Get your heart pumping; jog, run, or walk; keep your cholesterol low; get rid of that roll of fat; cut down on the bad fats, salt, and sugar; eat more fruits and vegetables; take your vitamins; the list of do's and don'ts is endless! There's no shortage of fitness centers where we can have a heart-healthy workout. Stores stock a mind-boggling array of products promising to make us healthier. Medical science advances on its quest to extend our life span. But I have news for you; Methuselah's age record is safe!

A few years ago, when oat bran was thought to reduce cholesterol, there was a joke about an elderly couple who died and went to heaven. When he saw how wonderful it was, the husband said to his wife: "We could have been here a lot sooner if you hadn't made us eat all that oat bran." Physical fitness is good – even if it delays our entrance into heaven. God expects us to treat our bodies well. I Corinthians 3:16-17 tells us we are God's temple in which His Spirit lives. But eternal life isn't attained on a treadmill. And physical life, however long, doesn't compare with the spiritual life God has planned for us (see I Timothy 4:8). Even physical fitness leads to a "dead end."

"Climb the ladder of success." – What is success? Does one have to reach the top of the ladder to achieve it"? The fact is; even if they reach the top rung, most people are unsatisfied. According to history, Alexander the Great cried because there were "no more worlds to conquer." Whether the goal is wealth or prestige or power, it's lonely at the top.

In a Blondie cartoon, by Young and Lebrun, Dagwood was asking his boss, Mr. Dithers, for a raise. As usual, Dithers wasn't responding favorably. "Dagwood," he said, "it's true you don't make much money. But you're young, strong, healthy, fit, and have a wonderful wife and children. I, on the other hand, have none of those things. To make up for it, I get lots of money. Now, I think that's fair, don't you?" But lots of money – or any other worldly success – cannot make up for the absence of life's higher values. So, climbing the success ladder is a dead end road – unless there is a bridge to a better life. But, thank God, there is one!

JESUS' TRANSFORMATION OF LIFE AND DEATH

We have someone, better qualified than the Texas gravedigger, to give us a true perspective on life and death. His name is Jesus. He's qualified because He knows what comes after death. He's the ultimate authority because of who He is. He's the very Source of life! Consider Creation; Jesus was there when it all happened. John 1:2-3 declares: "He was with God in the beginning. Through Him all things were made; without Him nothing was made that has been made." Then John adds (v. 4) "In Him was (and is) life. . ."

According to Genesis 1:31, when God completed His work of Creation, He was pleased with His work. But something went terribly wrong. Sin entered the world and destroyed the beauty of the life God planned. The sad result – we're all born with a fallen nature, spiritually dead (See Ephesians 2:1). According to Bible scholars, it was between 4 and 6 B.C. when God said, "It's time to do something about human depravity." So Jesus came to earth in a new role. This time He came as the re-creator of life. He came preaching "you must be born again." And then He died on a cross to make that possible.

The story of our salvation doesn't end at the Cross. The Holy Spirit was sent to empower Jesus' followers to live the holy life. 120 disciples obeyed their orders to wait for His coming. Ten days of waiting, praying, heart searching. In an "upper room." And it happened on the day of Pentecost. The Holy Spirit came upon them, filled them, and empowered them. They were fully spiritually alive. Thousands were converted. And Jesus' Church began its ministry to a sin-cursed world, as our Lord rejoiced – this time at His work of re-creation. And Jesus exclaimed, "Now, that's really livin'!"

Our Savior talked a lot about life. Check your concordance. You'll find many inspiring verses. We especially like the one about "abundant life" or "life to the full" (John 10:10). We all want the full life. Many years ago a beverage commercial advertised: "you only go around once in life, so you have to grab for all the gusto you can get." But the world's "gusto" is never quite enough. Jesus' full life is something more than the artificial "highs" of the world. Once, when I had preached a sermon in which I referred to the Christian lifestyle, a retired minister in the congregation gently chided me. He said: "I don't want a lifestyle; I want a life!" He was right. There's more to life than just "style".

A small boy was told to bring his birth certificate to school, but he forgot and left it at home. Arriving at his classroom, he apologized, "I'm sorry, teacher; I forgot my excuse for being born." So, what's my excuse for being born? What's yours? Why are we here? What's our purpose in life? The Christian's primary goal is to reach heaven. But, until we get there, we have a life to live. We can spend it or waste it, or we can invest it. The greatest use of life is to invest in something that will outlast it. That's the essence of Jesus' definition of a full life.

LIFE THROUGH DEATH

Jesus taught the death route to real life. That's the paradox of our life principle: "You have to die to really live." I don't like that principle. Do you? It sounds painful – and it is. We want life, not death. But the point is, real life is costly. Our eternal life cost Jesus dearly. Our sins crucified Him. We have the hope of heaven because He died for us. It's not hard to believe in that life through death principle, but it applies to our lives here, too. We, also, have some dying to do. And that's a bit more disturbing. We don't relish the thought of personal sacrifice.

In John 12:23-24, Jesus was preparing His disciples for His approaching death on the cross. He pointed out the necessity for a kernel of wheat to die in the ground in order to produce more wheat. It was an analogy of His coming death. But He didn't stop there. In verse 25, He indicated we, too, must be involved with death in order to produce life. The wonderful paradox is that out of our voluntary sacrifice we become what the Apostle Paul called a "living sacrifice". (Romans 12:1) I once heard a missionary describe how a witch doctor urged the natives to give a living sacrifice. It was to be an animal, which would be set free to roam, and it would be ready for the spirits to use at any time. Our sacrificial mission is to be available for the Holy Spirit's use at any time.

The apostle Paul wrote of his own experience of dying for a spiritual purpose: "I have been crucified with Christ, and I no longer live, but Christ lives in me." (Galatians 2:20) What a paradox! Crucified, yet alive – fully alive! It's a fact of life; we can't fully live until we're ready to die. That's true regarding our preparation for physical death and eternal life. But it's also true that we must die to some things of this world in order to have full life while we're on this earth. Some used to call it "dying out". Not a bad term. Perhaps it's even more meaningful to us than being "crucified with Christ".

Spiritual victory doesn't come from just "dying out" in the abstract. The death must be specific. In one sense it's a lifetime death; in another, it's a continuing process. There does need to be that moment when you surrender all to follow Christ. Call it entire sanctification, complete consecration, crucifixion with Christ – call it whatever you wish, it must be a lifetime commitment. A commitment to follow Him, wherever He leads. A commitment to allow the Holy Spirit to control and empower your life. A commitment to live a holy life, as the Holy Spirit enables you.

Whatever your spiritual attainments, you're still human. Life circumstances change. You experience new pressures and temptations. Age takes its toll on bodies and spirits. An old man in a nursing home declared, "If I had known I was going to live this long, I'd have taken better care of myself." At least he had maintained

a good sense of humor! God designed you to live forever with Him

in heaven; life demands spiritual maintenance here on earth. So,

like the apostle Paul, you need to "die daily" to anything that would

hinder you from reaching your goal.

THE DYING OUT LIST

Specifically, what is included in the "dying out" list? Actually,

the list must be very personal. But there are some things that should

appear on every list: sin, people, selfish aspirations, even life itself.

Heading the list is **sin**. Colossians 3:5 tells us to "put to

death. . . whatever belongs to your earthly (sinful) nature." In the

verses that follow Paul is pretty specific about what things need to

die. Our world treats sin so lightly. Even Christians normalize it,

rationalize it, and practice it without even a twinge of conscience.

But God doesn't dismiss willful sin with an indulgent nod. It's a

serious matter with Him. He calls on us to renounce ungodliness

and live holy lives. While discussing the subject of salvation by grace

through faith, Paul writes, "Shall we go on sinning so that grace may

increase? By no means! We died to sin; how can we live in it any

longer?" (Romans 6:1-2) Notice Paul says "we died to sin." If we are

truly dead to sin, it will make a difference in our lives. When we're

dead to sin we become fully alive to God. Now, that's life to the full!

Most find that, in order to experience spiritual victory, they have to die out to **people**; to what they say, what they do, what they don't do. Job experienced harsh criticism from his friends who came to sympathize and stayed to criticize. Whoever said "sticks and stones may break my bones, but words can never harm me" was either deaf or delirious. Human relationships frequently bring pain. But there's alleviation of that pain when we die out to the words and actions of others in order to rest in God's grace.

Life goals and aspirations are important, but they must not be allowed to dominate our lives. So, in a real sense we need to die out to them. A man purchased a cemetery lot and had a gravestone placed there. He was questioned about its inscription: "Born a human being; died a wholesale grocer." He explained, "I was so busy selling groceries I didn't have time to marry and have a family. I was so busy I never had time to live."

Everyone makes mistakes. And that brings regrets. Often we wish we could live our lives over. But we can't. And there's no guarantee we'd do any better the second time around. Here's a better plan: Trust God that He really does "blot out our transgressions" – large and small. . . that He does take the ugly ashes of wasted years and miraculously transforms them into something of eternal beauty. It's all through His amazing grace and our acceptance of it. Now, that's "really livin!"

Applying the Principle – Discussion Questions

1. How can we keep from being controlled by a fast pace of life?

2. What are signs that "things own you"?

3. How do you define "success"?

4. What is the difference between a lifestyle and a life?

5. How does your Christian faith affect your attitude toward death?

6. What does being "dead to sin" mean to you?

7. In addition to reaching heaven, what are some worthwhile life goals?

CHAPTER 2

ATTITUDE IS MORE IMPORTANT THAN ALTITUDE

Let's suppose you are piloting an airplane. You've left the relative security of earth. You're flying, hundreds or thousands of feet high. Your plane is held aloft by the rush of unseen air under and above its' wings. You're committed to moving forward; there's no reverse gear. You can't stop; you know if you stop you'll drop. Among the instruments in front of you is one that tells your altitude – how high you're flying. That's important to know; it helps you avoid hitting trees and towers and mountains.

There's another word that's important to pilots. The word is "attitude". In aviation terminology, it refers to the horizontal direction of the aircraft. It describes whether it is headed up or down. The plane may be flying miles above earth, but if the direction is downward – even slightly – it will eventually crash. And so, for you as the pilot, attitude is even more important than altitude.

Most likely, you are not a pilot. You've never flown a plane, and you don't expect to take flying lessons anytime soon. But the same principle applies to your journey through life. Let's state the principle in another way: where you are headed is more important than where you are. In a contest between destination and location, destination wins – hands down! If you're headed in the wrong direction, your location is pretty irrelevant.

Let's come back to the word "attitude". It's a powerful word – not only for aviators, but also for landlubbers like you and me. Your attitude is your battleground for dealing with life. It's a mindset that either enables you to cope with life or sends you on a downward spiral to defeat.

Sometimes life seems to be a bummer. You work your fingers to the bone, and it seems all you get is bony fingers. A teacher was lecturing her class on the value of industriousness. "Now, children," she said, "there's a wonderful example in the life of the ant. He keeps busy every day. And, in the end, what happens to him?" A child in the back of the room answered: "Someone steps on him." In the drama of life, just when you think you're getting your act together, the curtain comes down. Probably you've experienced enough of life's struggles and frustrations and heartaches that you agree life isn't easy. People lose their jobs; tragedies happen; loved ones die; disease destroys bodies; injustices occur.

Once a friend told me he had discussed his problems with someone, and he was advised to cheer up; things could be worse. So, he cheered up, and sure enough, things got worse! Most of us have had similar experiences. Circumstances don't always improve. Sometimes they do get worse. Maybe comforting words can't ease the pain, but attitude can. After losing the presidential election to Dwight Eisenhower, Adlai Stevenson joked, "I'm too old to cry, and it hurts too much to laugh."

Sydney J. Harris put things into perspective in his book, Majority of One, when he wrote: "When I hear somebody sigh, 'Life is hard', I'm tempted to ask, 'Compared to what'?" It's true; life can be hard. But attitude can make it easier. Or harder. Attitude will eventually reveal itself in some kind of action. A positive attitude may not destroy the scorpion of stress, but it can remove its' stinger. The Apostle Paul had a long list of bad circumstances, but he wrote, "I have learned to be content whatever the circumstances." (Philippians 4:11) What an attitude! It enabled him to write, ". . . we also rejoice in our suffering, because we know that suffering produces perseverance; perseverance, character; and character, hope. And hope does not disappoint us. . ." (Romans 5:3-5) That is attitude working in a positive way.

"Nevertheless" is a Powerful Word

Some time ago, I discovered what I call "The Nevertheless Principle." It's not original with me. Jesus practiced it in Gethsemane when He prayed, ". . . nevertheless, not as I will, but as thou wilt." (Matthew 26:39 KJV) He taught it to Simon Peter on two occasions, one near the beginning and the other at the end of His ministry on earth. In Luke 5, we read of Jesus calling the first disciples to follow Him. Peter was one of them. That morning his fishing boat became a floating platform for Jesus' teaching ministry. That was fine with Peter. But when he was told to go out into deep water and let down the nets, he protested: "Master, we've worked hard all night and haven't caught anything!" You can't blame him for objecting. After all, he was a professional fisherman. He knew the lake like the back of his hand. He knew the fish just weren't there. But, to his credit, Peter passed this obedience test. His reply, in the KJV (verse 5) gives us the key word in this principle: "Nevertheless, at your word, I will let down the nets." Peter closed his eyes to negative circumstances and opened his eyes to positive faith in Jesus. This response is far more significant than the resulting huge catch of fish that broke the nets and sank two boats.

The second lesson, recorded in John 21, also took place at the lakeshore. It was after Jesus' death and resurrection. Peter and the other disciples had gone back to fishing. Again their luck was bad. No fish. Jesus' instructions were simple; just throw the nets on the other side of the boat. This time Peter didn't protest. He was learning The Principle. But there was one more lesson to come.

When Jesus prophesied Peter would die as a martyr for his faith, jealousy reared its ugly head. "Well, what about John; will he die a martyr, too?" Jesus' reply (verse 22) drove the lesson home: "If I want him to remain alive until I return, what is that to you? You must follow me." The book of Acts proves Peter finally saw the light! He joined the rest of the 120 waiting in the Upper Room. He experienced Pentecost. He became a spiritual giant in the Church. And the Nevertheless Principle helped him become the man his Lord saw in him.

Here's an obvious meaning, for us, of Peter's lessons: nothing should be allowed to keep us from following Jesus. Life puts many barriers in our way. Remember: we can't do it just on a because of basis; we must also live our lives in spite of some circumstances. That's the secret of coping with life's roadblocks.

Practicing "Nevertheless" Living

It would be nice if this attitude came automatically. But it doesn't. For most of us it requires some effort and discipline. Here are some suggestions:

Remember your past blessings and victories. There's a little poem, written by someone unknown to me, that beautifully expresses the fact that our past can help us cope with today:

There was a dachshund once,

So long he hadn't any notion

How long it took to notify

His tail of his emotion.

And so it was that when his eyes

Were filled with tears of sadness

His little tail went wagging on

Because of previous gladness.

You and I don't need wagging tails, but we do need cheerful hearts. And, like the little dog in the poem, our "previous gladness" can help us have a present joy that outlasts bad circumstances. But what about the bad memories? Well, when we're struggling to cope with difficult circumstances, that's the time to practice "selective memory". Focus on the good thoughts of the past, not the bad ones. It takes discipline, but it improves attitude!

Don't fall into the comparison trap. Human comparisons can get you into trouble. Some of it is normal and necessary in human relationships. Examples are athletic competition, academic scores, and job performance. There's a natural tendency to look down on those who make us look good and to resent those who make us look bad. And that's not good. But comparing life circumstances with others is downright dangerous. So, don't compare yourself with others; make Jesus your role model. He would say to you: "don't let

the lucky breaks of others – or your misfortunes – get you down."
When things in your life go sour and it seems unfair, you may or not
be getting a "raw deal". But, regardless, by saying a sanctified "so
what", you practice the Nevertheless Principle.

In II Corinthians 10:12, Paul counsels against the comparison
trap: "We do not dare to classify or compare ourselves with some
who commend themselves. When they measure themselves by
themselves and compare themselves with themselves, they are not
wise." Then, in verse 18, he gives the reason for his warning: "For it
is not the one who commends himself who is approved, but the one
whom the Lord commends."

Refuse to be a negative person. You may be prone to feel
sorry for yourself occasionally. Perhaps that's normal. Many Bible
characters had their negative moments: Moses, David, Job, Elijah,
John the Baptist, to name a few. Even Jesus, dying on the cross, cried
out, " my God, my God, why have you forsaken me?" (Mark 15:34)
While this was more of an exclamation than a question, it reveals
the depth of His human emotions. So don't get down on yourself if
you yield to a small pity party occasionally. But refuse to allow such
negative thoughts to persist, take control, and dominate your whole
outlook on life. Refuse to dwell on life's injustices; just live justly,
yourself.

Someone has observed that an optimist thinks the glass is half full, while a pessimist thinks the glass is half-empty. A realist, on the other hand, knows that if he sticks around, he's eventually going to have to wash the glass. I disagree with that assessment. I believe you can be a realist without having a negative view of life. But, for some , it may require an attitude adjustment.

Live by God's formula. Micah 6:8 tells us what it is: "And what does the Lord require of you? To act justly and to love mercy and to walk humbly with your God."

"act justly" -- that's behaving the way we believe.

"love mercy" – that's putting the love of Christ into our action.

"*walk humbly with. . . God*" – that's making God # 1 in our lives.

Micah's prescription shifts the focus from what's wrong in our lives to what we can do to make things right in someone else's life. In a recent Reflecting God devotional, Merritt Nielson stated: "Justice says, 'You're only getting what you deserve.' Mercy announces, 'You won't be getting what you deserve'." The miracle is that when we care more about God and others, we can better cope with our own pain.

A nine-year old boy named Darrell was horribly burned in a fire that killed four members of his family. Someone heard him screaming in pain, as the dressings were being changed, and loudly exclaimed, "How can God do this to an innocent child?" Darrell heard the question and answered, "Don't say anything against God! When it hurts, God cries with me." That's the Nevertheless Principle at work.

Some events in life have no logical explanation. So don't think you have to understand everything that happens. The fact is: we're slow learners. Peter was. It took many lessons before he grasped this truth. The two fishing lessons (Luke 5 and John 21). . . .The Transfiguration experience. . . His denial and restoration. . . The Resurrection. Finally, emptied of his sinful self and filled with the Holy Spirit, he was ready for unquestioning obedience.

The message for you and me: trust and obey – even if we don't understand the circumstances or the orders. The Principle needs to work in our lives 24/7, not just on special occasions. Life's personal losses make us either better or bitter, depending on our attitude. Concerning a committed Christian who had suffered many heartbreaking losses, it was said, "When he could not enjoy the faith of assurance, he held on with the faith of adherence." God give us the simple yet complete faith revealed by a small child who unhesitatingly jumps into the outstretched arms of his father!

Someone once made this profound observation: "I can't change the direction of the wind, but I can adjust my sails to always reach my destination." Some things in life we can change; others we cannot. May we have the good sense to know the difference. And may we keep committed to reaching our destination – in spite of all obstacles.

Remember: attitude – where you're headed – is more

important than altitude – where you are.

Applying the Principle – Discussion Questions

1. What factors influence your attitudes?

2. How do you define contentment?

3. Why do some Christians have a "bad attitude"?

4. What helps you keep from being defeated by bad memories?

5. Is it ever alright to compare yourself with another human being? Under what circumstances?

6. Are some people "negative" by nature?

7. Is it better to receive mercy or give mercy?

CHAPTER 3

THERE IS STRENGTH IN WEAKNESS

Someone has pointed out that, while the world rewards short-term success, God rewards long-term faithfulness. The world is impressed by musical talent, physical ability, cosmetic beauty, muscular handsomeness, eloquent words. God is impressed by what's in the heart. Multi-million dollar salaries, adulation of adoring fans, performance awards – these are the rewards of the world. But God has a different opinion of success. His rewards may be less visible, but they are more real. From the eternal perspective, many of the world's achievements are just "much ado about nothing". Records are made, only to be broken by someone else. Stars fall in the popularity charts. Everyone's wealth eventually is left behind.

There is a natural human desire to achieve, to rise above the ordinary. That desire is God-given. He approves of our achieving excellence. It's fundamentally good. NBA coach Pat Riley says "excellence is the gradual result of always striving to do better." This should make life better for all. It's a powerful motivating force. Talk show host Rush Limbaugh has stated that "80 % of achievement is passion (or desire)." The problem is that too often that passion is misdirected. Many discover that, after they have climbed the ladder of success, it's leaning against the wrong wall. And that's a real tragedy. It happens because people think they know what's best for them. But they don't. Only God does. And He wants to help them reach that goal.

Achievement Goals

Before we consider how to get there, let's look at some goals that are appropriate for a committed Christian:

Success – Someone has said a man is a success when he is the man his mother thinks he is and the man his mother-in-law wishes he were. As humorous as that definition may be, it's an improvement over the measurement by wealth or prestige. Our motivation for achieving must come from something deeper than the desire for profit, prestige or power. Otherwise, we live without morals, ethics, or compassion.

In an article on "Cheating", in the March, 2006, issue of Reader's Digest, Gay Jervey writes: ". . . two forces are behind the erosion in ethics. First, advances in technology – chiefly the Internet and portable digital devices – have made cheating easier. A bigger factor, though, is the way bad behavior across society – ballplayers popping steroids, business executives cooking corporate books, journalists fabricating quotes, even teachers faking test scores to make schools look good – signals that nothing is out of bounds when success is at stake." What a tragedy when the end is used to justify any means! We cannot measure success in this life without considering its' eternal implications. God is more concerned about people than possessions; He cares more about our character than our performance. And His opinion of our "success" is what's most important. So, strive for success. Just make sure God approves of the goal.

Security – It's such an elusive goal. Just when you think you have it, it disappears. A few years ago a 60 year- old man was struck and killed by his radio-controlled model airplane when he was blinded by the sun. Ironically, he had quit drag racing because he thought it was too dangerous. That's life. Sometimes good choices bring bad results. It's impossible to avoid all risk. One day you're sitting on top of the world; the next day your world is falling apart. Employment, relationships, financial resources, physical health – all these are vulnerable to loss of security.

The desire for security is normal. It's God-given. It's a basic human need. And that same God also created us with the desire for achievement. Here's our dilemma: achieving usually involves some risk-taking – the very opposite of security. At the very least, we have to leave our comfort zone. I believe God approves of risk-taking, as well as security, if it's for a worthwhile purpose. So how do we balance these opposite desires? The obvious answer is to allow God to help us. He will temper our drive for accomplishment, molding and shaping it into conformity with His will. And He will be our source of security. Not life in a bubble of isolation from the real world. No guarantee that we'll have all profit and no loss. No promise that we'll never have to face sickness or death. Just the assurance of God's awesome presence. Leading. Guiding. Protecting. Supporting. Restoring. The shepherd-king David described it beautifully in Psalm 23. Now, that's security we can count on!

Fulfillment – An airline pilot remarked to his co-pilot, "See that lake below us? When I was a boy, I fished in that lake and dreamed of someday flying a plane. Now I fly over the lake and dream of the day when I can be fishing there again." Probably there's no such thing as total fulfillment. Life could always be better in some way. And the human spirit is impatient with adverse circumstances. But we can find fulfillment even when we wish things were different. And that's essential for satisfying achievement.

In <u>Catholic Digest</u>, Bette Howland wrote: "For a long time it seemed to me that real life was about to begin, but there was always some obstacle in the way. Something had to be got through first, some unfinished business, time still to be served, a debt to be paid. Then life would begin. At last it dawned on me that these obstacles were my life." She had started on the path to fulfillment. She had come to terms with her circumstances. Her obstacles were transformed into opportunities; her defeats into victories; her dreams into visions.

Self-fulfillment is the term most frequently used. While many give it too much importance, it is a fundamental need. It's what's in our hearts that counts. Life's most valuable possession is what's inside us. And your real need is fulfillment in the "real you". Not the social you or the emotional you or the vocational you – but the "you" that can be known only in your heart. The real issue is this: what brings you fulfillment, satisfaction, and happiness? Maybe an attitude adjustment is needed. The apostle Paul said he had *learned* to be content whatever the circumstances (Philippians 4:11) You can learn to keep fulfilled within even when your life is in turmoil. Someone has observed: "even times of sorrow are valuable – they help us recognize when we are happy." You can learn to enjoy the scenery even when taking a detour. You can learn to enjoy things without having to acquire them.

Then there's God-fulfillment. In the AFA Journal, February, 1993, Don Wildman wrote, "the goal in life is not happiness, as many seem to think. The goal of life is holiness. Living your life in the will of God. Investing your life in something which will outlive you. Contributing to those who have preceded and those who will follow you." It has been said that there is a God-shaped hole in our hearts until He fills it with Himself. It's also true that fulfillment is empty until He is a part of it. In John 1:16 we read: "From the fullness of his grace we have all received one blessing after another." That's the foundation of real fulfillment!

Christlikeness – Last Sunday for the offertory, our church orchestra played "I'd Rather Have Jesus." I closed my eyes and I could almost hear George Beverly Shea's rich baritone voice resonating the words at a Billy Graham Crusade. And then I thought: "I don't want to just *have* Jesus; I want to *be like* Jesus." And that should be the primary goal of every Christian. For many years I carried in my billfold a promise card which read: "If you could see yourself the man God meant, you nevermore would be the man you are, content." As a senior adult, I'm still challenged by that statement. According to Paul, a vital part of the church's mission is to help Christians ". . . become mature, attaining to the whole measure of the fullness of Christ." (Ephesians 4:13) And that's a goal worth striving for.

Achieving the Goals

We don't like to admit weakness. We'd rather whistle when it's dark; put on a happy face when in a crowd; let a smile be an umbrella when life is stormy. We bravely keep a stiff upper lip when our spirits are sagging. When someone asks how we're doing, we glibly reply "just fine". But there is a point at which our strength will fail. Then, in life's extremity, we reach out for God's opportunity.

Someone has said, "When you have nothing left but God, then, for the first time, you realize God is enough."

It's good to face your weakness and take hold of God's strength when you are down and out. But I would suggest a better plan. While you are still "on top of your world", accept your limitations and form a partnership with the God of unlimited power. Don't wait for life to force you to face your weakness.

What a privilege to be **in partnership with God!** There's an old fable about an elephant and a mouse crossing a bridge together. After they reached the far side, the mouse said to his friend, "We sure shook that bridge, didn't we!" Obviously, the shaking of the bridge came, not from the mouse, but from his pachyderm partner. Sorry to tell you, but in your partnership with God, you're the mouse. Together, you and God can shake the world. But the real power comes from God. As Paul wrote, in I Corinthians 1:25, ". . . the weakness of God is stronger than man's strength."

Does this mean our role is unimportant? Certainly not! As someone advised, "trust God to move your mountain, but keep on climbing." We know He created the world, but He also chose to work with humans to accomplish His purposes in that world. Jesus told His disciples "anyone who has faith in me will do what I have been doing. He will do *even greater things than these* because I am going to the Father." (John 14:12) "Greater things than Jesus"

– that's mind boggling! It's possible only because of the partnership. Your greatest achievements occur when you and God work as a team.

A motivational speaker named Denis Waitley challenged his audience by saying, "Your greatest achievement is to outperform yourself." No doubt, in his mind, that meant to stretch yourself beyond your perceived limits. That's good advice. Dependence on God is no excuse for failing to do your very best. In <u>Go for the Goal</u>, famed soccer player Mia Hamm wrote, "Celebrate what you've accomplished, but raise the bar a little each time you succeed." You never really test the power of God until you attempt something beyond your own resources.

The Apostle Paul knew something about human weakness. He was afflicted with what he described as "a thorn in the flesh". (I Corinthians 12:7) He repeatedly prayed for Gods healing touch, but it never came. Instead, the Lord told him, "my grace is sufficient for you, for my power is made perfect in weakness." Paul understood, and he responded, "Therefore I will boast all the more gladly about my weaknesses, so that Christ's power may rest on me. That's why, for Christ's sake, I delight in weaknesses, in insults, in hardships, in persecutions, in difficulties. For *when I am weak, then I am strong.*" There's our principle for achieving: there is strength in weakness – when it is surrendered to God.

In Ephesians 6:10, we're instructed to be "strong in the Lord and in His mighty power." Then, verse 13 tells us to put on the "full armor of God". A list of the armor follows. Paul told us to put these things on; he understood God doesn't do for us what we should do for ourselves. Our weakness becomes strength as we use the resources He provides. We're called to be partners with God in life's battles, not idle bystanders.

So how can we best fulfill our role as "junior partners?" A good starting place is to **remove the hindrances.** Hebrews 12:1 admonishes us to ". . . throw off everything that hinders and the sin that so easily entangles, and let us run with perseverance the race marked out for us." Some subtractions need to occur in our lives in order for God to add His full power through us. In the journey of life, it's better to remove the stone from our shoe than limp along uncomfortably. Obviously, deliberate sin needs to go. But there are many other "stones" that need to be removed. Think about your own life; is there a stone that's causing a limp?

There's a challenging admonition in Ephesians 5:16: "Be very careful how you live, making the best use of your time (Phillips) and every opportunity (NIV)." This requires personal discipline. God won't do it for you. We're tempted to waste our time and energy on things that don't really matter. Most of us have **too much clutter in our lives.** We need an occasional spiritual housecleaning. Life is measured, not merely by what we get done, but also by what we purposely leave undone. Time management people tell us to reduce to habit everything possible. That's good advice. It can reduce one's stress level and increase effectiveness. Just make sure the habits are good ones.

For many years, churches have been trying to help their people discover their spiritual gifts. That's a good starting point. But it's of little value unless those gifts and talents are used faithfully and effectively. So, don't bury your talent; invest it – in your partnership with God.

A long time ago the Psalmist wrote, "This is the day the Lord has made; let us rejoice and be glad in it." (Psalm 118:24) God wants positive, happy, optimistic partners in His Kingdom work. There are times when sorrow and sadness are inescapable. But we need not live under such a cloud continually. After all, "we know that in all things God works for the good of those who love Him. . ." (Romans 8:28) What a spirit-lifting promise! In all things – God is working in our behalf. Every day. All day long. Taking bad circumstances and ultimately transforming them into something good. And, by our attitude, we, too, can do something positive to transform our lives. So, **focus on the positive!**

Think of each day as a miniature lifetime. A lady named Cathy Better wrote the following beautiful essay on living our days to the full:

"Each day that we awake is a new start, another chance.

Why waste it on self-pity, sloth and selfishness?

Roll that day around on your tongue; relish the taste of its freedom.

Breathe deeply of the morning air, savor the fragrance of opportunity.

Run your hands along the spine of those precious 24 hours;

Feel the strength in that sinew and bone.

Life is the raw material; we are the artisans.

We can sculpt our existence into something beautiful or debase it into ugliness.

It's in our hands."

Although we, in ourselves, are weak, God has delegated to us, His partners, this awesome power. That's amazing!

Let me suggest a very important achievement goal: seek to have God's perspective on life. That's not easy. He is omnipotent; we are finite. He is divine; we are human. He is all-knowing; we know so little. He views life on earth from heaven; we try to understand heavenly life from earth. But we're partners, so we need to be in agreement. How can this happen? I believe the only way is through the indwelling Presence of the Holy Spirit. Shortly before His crucifixion, Jesus told His disciples He would send the Holy Spirit to fill their lives with God's Presence. And He promised, "When He, the Spirit of Truth comes, He will guide you into all truth." (John 16:13) That's the secret –- God's Spirit within us makes the partnership work. His wisdom, His love, His grace – yes, even His power are channeled through us as we yield our weaknesses and our strengths to His control.

In his book, See You at the Top, Zig Ziglar writes "What you get by reaching your destination isn't nearly as important as what you become while reaching it." Yes, in ourselves we are weak. But through our partnership with God we have strength that's "out of this world"!

Applying the Principle – Discussion Questions

1. What would you most like to achieve during your lifetime?

2. What is your biggest obstacle to achievement?

3. How do you know when you have achieved success?

4. How can we get rid of the life "clutter" that hinders us?

5. Which goal is more important to you: security or success?

6. What gives you the greatest fulfillment in life?

7. Can you think of a time when the Holy Spirit gave you specific guidance?

CHAPTER 4

HISTORY DOESN'T DETERMINE DESTINY

Several years ago, a young pastor was invited to speak to the convicts at a federal penitentiary. Concerned about how he would be received, he nervously approached the platform. Walking up the steps, he tripped and fell flat on the floor. The prison walls rang with laughter. With a flash of inspiration the minister got up, strode to the podium, and exclaimed, "Men, that's exactly why I'm here – to tell you a man may fall down, but he can get up again!"

Probably you've never been a prisoner. But you know something about failure. Here's the good news: just because you've written a bad chapter or two, that doesn't have to ruin your life story. The fact is, most failures are not monumental events. More often, they are simply routine instances of "messing up" in some life situation. Failure need not be final. That's the message of our Principle: "History Doesn't Determine Destiny." What you do with today and tomorrow is more important than what you did yesterday.

Failure can strike you from many directions. It might be financial, in either business or personal finances. It might come through your humanity in mistakes or bad judgment. It might occur in a competitive situation, such as athletics or academics. It could happen in your home as marital or child-rearing failure. It's possible it could be the result of a character flaw, revealed in moral or ethical failure. And it could be a spiritual failure – either in doing or being. But however you experience it, it's not defeat unless you give up. Failure is an event, not a person. Don't personalize it by surrendering to it.

Since our subject is recovery from failure, you might be hoping for some profound formula. Some magic wand that would make the downfall just disappear. Sorry, that's not going to happen. As Beverly Sills, of the Metropolitan Opera, once commented: "There are no shortcuts to any place worth going." In the Calvin and Hobbes cartoon strip, by Bill Watterson, Calvin says to his buddy: "I feel bad that I called Suzie names and hurt her feelings. I'm sorry I did it." Hobbes replies, "Well, maybe you should apologize to her." Calvin ponders a moment, then responds, "I keep hoping there's a less obvious solution."

The steps I'm suggesting are pretty evident. No great wisdom from a brilliant mind. Most of the steps are simply practical, rather than spiritual. Yet God wants to help you recover. He does not see you as a failure. He sees you as the success you can be. So let Him walk with you on the path to recovery. The Psalmist testified of his experience: "My flesh and my heart may fail, but God is the strength of my heart. . ." (Psalm 73:26)   And He wants to strengthen *your* heart.

Put Your Failure into Perspective

"Misery loves company." Probably you've heard that all your life. Maybe that's true, maybe it's not. But it is true that it helps to remember failure is not abnormal. It's common. In fact, it happens to everyone. Including politicians. An unsuccessful candidate in a rural community reported he drove over 24,000 miles, was dog-bitten 6 times, joined 3 churches, was baptized twice by immersion, sprinkled 3 times, and poured once. He shelled 4 bushels of corn, hoed 13 rows of beans, and picked 2 bales of cotton. He kissed 126 babies, proposed to 3 widows, and still lost the election.

Every generation has its' famous success stories. We remember these people for their extraordinary accomplishments. But most of them were simply successful failures. Ty Cobb is famous as baseball's greatest base-stealer. But he was thrown out more times than anyone in baseball history. Babe Ruth, the home run king, struck out more times than any other major leaguer. Hank Aaron, who broke Ruth's record, also was a leading strikeout victim. Enrico Caruso became was one of the world's greatest tenor vocalists. But, as a music student, his voice so often failed to carry the high notes his voice teacher advised him to quit. Thomas Edison's teacher called him a dunce. But, after failing thousands of times, he finally succeeded in perfecting the incandescent light. When in school, both Albert Einstein and Werner von Braun flunked courses in math. (Source: <u>See You at the Top</u>, by Zig Ziglar) A more recent "successful failure" is Gary Heavin, the founder of the Curves physical fitness chain for women. Before finally succeeding, he went bankrupt and lost everything, including his marriage. So, why do we remember these men as success stories? Because they recovered from their failures.

The Scriptures also tell us of some great people who failed miserably. There was Abraham, the father of God's "chosen nation". Read about God's covenant with him, in Genesis, chapters 12 and 15. A man of great faith. But he failed the Hagar test. David, the shepherd-boy, became "a man after (God's) own heart." (I Samuel 13:14) But he had repeated failures – most notoriously his adultery with Bathsheba. Peter, the big fisherman, was a member of Jesus' inner circle. Bold, impulsive, and powerful. Yet, he, too, failed. After courageously defending Jesus in the Garden of Betrayal, he wilted before a servant girl. Denied he even knew Jesus – three times. (Mark 14:66-72) John Mark, author of the second Gospel, knew about Peter's failure. Even wrote about it. But that didn't keep him from his own failure. As a promising young missionary with Paul and Barnabas, he bailed out in Pamphilia. Went home to mama. (Acts 15:37-38)

There are dark chapters in the biographies of Abraham,

David, Peter, and Mark, So why do we consider them great men? Because they, too, recovered from their failures. Remember: there's a big difference between experiencing failure and *being* a failure. True for them; true for you. However you failed, you can recover. You can learn from their failures and successes. In fact, you need to. You won't live long enough to make all of life's mistakes yourself! And you need to learn from their example of experiencing God's grace of recovery.

Someone has pointed out that failure comes before success – in the dictionary and in life. So, when post-failure emotions get you down, keep this in mind: success is only one step beyond failure. Recovery may be closer then you think.

Refuse to Bury Your Head in the Sand

Pity the poor ostrich. Rightly or wrongly, he bears the stigma of burying his head in the sand when in a threatening situation. That can be a temptation when you fail. Perhaps it's because of embarrassment. A pretty normal reaction. It's hard to face other people. You're worried about "looking bad" in their eyes. Or maybe it's a sign of the wrong kind of pride. Proverbs 16:18 says, "Pride goes. . . before a fall." And it follows you after a fall! It can be a problem after success, too.

Someone has said, "the two hardest things to handle in life are failure and success." Pride is a major barrier to recovery. Make sure you don't ignore the failure because of it. And don't put your head in the sand because you don't want to face your failure. If an apology is warranted, give it; if forgiveness is needed, ask for it; if restitution is called for, make it. If sin needs confessed, do it to God, and repent with all your heart.

Here's an encouraging observation: "It takes as much courage to have tried and failed as it does to have tried and succeeded." Without being arrogantly proud, keep your head erect and your shoulders straight. One man testified: "I'm never down; I'm either up or I'm getting up." What a good attitude! It will help you keep your head out of the sand and your eyes on Jesus. And He will help you on your road to recovery.

Don't Play the Blame Game

It's not unusual for athletes to try to cover their failure with a good act of injury. It's called "loser's limp". A baseball player misjudges a fly ball, so he trips and falls down. It wasn't his fault he failed to make the catch; something made him fall. A runner is losing the race, so he begins hobbling along the track. The problem wasn't his lack of speed or endurance; it was a muscle cramp. Somehow, they think it makes the failure more respectable if the blame is placed somewhere else.

Let's not be too hard on athletes. The "blame game" is commonly played by non-athletes, too. Irresponsibility is rampant throughout society. It's not just little children who plead "it's not my fault!" Probably most of us are guilty of a "loser's limp" performance occasionally. But we need to remember this: while it may soothe our injured pride, it does nothing to help us along the road to recovery from failure. But accepting responsibility does!

Stop Thinking Failure

Motivational speaker Zig Ziglar has a colorful term for negative thinking. He calls it "stinkin' thinkin'". It will take over your thoughts if you don't resist. Especially when you're discouraged by some failure. Quaint fatalistic sayings are common in casual conversation:

"You can't teach an old dog new tricks."

"Whatever will be, will be."

"You made your bed; now you have to lie in it."

One of Murphy's laws: "If anything can go wrong, it will."

"You reap what you sow."

You could add others to that list. While each has an element of truth, they all program our minds toward failure. And that's bad. You won't experience recovery by practicing "stinkin' thinkin'".

If you have faced up to your failure, put it behind you. Learn from it, but don't keep re-living it. It's a part of your history, not your destiny. Don't let your mind dwell on it. But there's a broader application of our principle. Don't think failure. Period. Don't have a negative mindset. Nutritionists tell us: "You are what you eat." It's even more true that you are what you think. Proverbs 23:7 (KJV) says, "As a man thinks in his heart, so is he." Bible scholars say this is not a good translation of the Hebrew text. But it is a good description of what controls most human actions.

A fisherman was seen throwing back the large fish and keeping the small ones. When asked the reason, he replied, "The big ones won't fit in my frying pan." Don't let the size of your skillet determine the size of your catch! Plan for success. As someone has said, "to fail to plan is to plan to fail."

Dream a New Dream

Failure may diminish your dream or may even destroy it. If that happens, you need to build a new one. Don't be afraid to dream. Not the kind you have when you're snoozing in your bed. But the kind you need when you're wide awake and struggling to escape the valley of discouragement. They're needed for recovery from failure. Some need to be replaced; some renewed; some adjusted. But all need to be fresh. God considers them important. In Joel 2:28, dreams and visions are connected with the outpouring of God's Spirit on His people. And His Spirit working in you will generate fresh vision for your life journey.

Martin Luther King, Jr. changed our world with his "I Have a Dream" speech. And you can change your world with a fresh vision of what you want to accomplish. Dreams are the life-blood of success. Add a committed heart that pumps the energizing force and you're on your way to recovery. You have what Dr. Robert Schuller calls "possibility thinking". Then you understand the same letters that spell *impossible* also can spell *I'm possible.*

As citizens of our capitalistic society, we believe in determination and hard work. Rightly so. But King Solomon said, "Where there is no vision, the people perish." (Proverbs 29:18 KJV) An old adage tells us to "keep our nose to the grindstone." But if that's all you do, as someone with a wry sense of humor pointed out, you'll just end up with a worn out grindstone and a very sore nose.

Rick Warren's book, The Purpose Driven Life, has struck a responsive chord in multitudes of hearts. We realize the need of something more than superficial desires. Life is serious business. We need to clarify our life purpose to give substance to our dreams. There's an old fable about a dog that boasted of his ability as a runner. One day he chased a rabbit but failed to catch it. Naturally, the other dogs teased him about his failure. His response: "Remember, the rabbit was running for his life. I was merely running for the fun of catching him."

Recovering from failure is not a fun run. We are literally running for our lives. Recovery is crucial. Does dreaming a new dream guarantee we'll never fail again? Certainly not. But, as an unknown poet wrote:

> "I've dreamed many dreams that never came true;
>
> I've seen them vanish at dawn.
>
> But I've re'lized enough of my dreams, thank God,
>
> To make me want to dream on."

Start Again – From Where You Are

Louisa Fletcher Tarkington once wrote, "Oh, I wish there were some wonderful place called the Land of Beginning Again, where all our mistakes and all our heartaches could be dropped like a shabby old coat, at the door, and never put on again." Here's the good news: there is! Today is the first day of the rest of your life. It's true you can't escape the consequences of past failures. But every day presents the opportunity of a fresh new beginning.

Here's the key: you have to *start where you are.* You can't go back where you were before you failed. And you can't magically transport yourself to where you wish to be. You may have to start with "baby steps". Perhaps you'll have to step into uncharted territory. Maybe leave your comfort zone. Several years ago, following an ice storm, I saw birds fluttering around our feeder. They were unable to get the food because of the ice. They left, hungry. However, the other side of the feeder had no ice, and the food was readily available. A good lesson for us! Often it's only a small step from failure to success.

Release Your Failure to God

The Global Positioning System (GPS) is an amazing technological development. The process that enables the satellite eye in the sky to track the location of vehicles blows my mind. But God's system is far superior. He not only knows where you are, He knows what's happening in your life: your hurts, your disappointments, your failures --- as well as your successes. And He cares deeply. He wants to heal your failures, calm your troubled waters, and guide you on the best path of life. But you need to release it all to Him.

Failure must not be allowed to "break one's spirit". However, releasing the failure to God brings a healing broken-ness that allows Him to transform bad circumstances into something good. Even tragedies provide opportunities for God to show His love and grace. It has been said that only broken lives are really useful to God. What a paradox! But it's possible only because God has the power to restore broken spirits.

George MacDonald once said: "God will help us when we cannot walk, and He will help us when we find it hard to walk, but He cannot help us if we will not walk." Talk to Him about your failure. Let Him share your pain. Leave your history behind. Then get on with your recovery. Remember: your history is not your destiny!

Applying the Principle – Discussion Questions

1. What is your biggest obstacle to facing up to failure?

2. What do you feel is the first step in recovery from failure?

3. What have you found most helpful in recovering from a failure?

4. In what way has failure made you a stronger person?

5. What kind of failure is most harmful to God's Kingdom?

6. What are some examples of "loser's limp" in non-athletic areas of life?

7. How does one determine if his or her "dreams and visions" have God's approval?

CHAPTER 5

YOU'RE MORE BLESSED IN GIVING THAN IN RECEIVING

It's Christmas Eve or Christmas morning (depending on your family tradition). You and your loved ones are gathered around the tree and the colorfully wrapped treasures beneath it. The ooh's and ah's echo throughout the room. The pile of wrapping paper clutter mounts. Children try out their new toys. Teens and adults happily hold up their new clothes and gadgets and gift cards. Appropriate gratitude is expressed. The annual family Christmas exchange brings warm hearts and happy emotions.

Two classes of people are present at this special event: givers and receivers. Actually, in most cases, it's the same people; just different roles. Which act brings the greatest satisfaction – giving or receiving? The prevailing attitude of the world is that it's better to receive. You see that in the current gambling craze; in the excitement over winning the lottery; in the court battles over inheritance; in compensation disputes between employers and employees. People want "their fair share" – plus a little more. Giving takes second place to receiving. But genuine inner satisfaction comes from giving more

53

than from receiving. God created us to live that way. And life is hollow if we live by another standard.

Whether or not you believe in Darwin's theory of the "survival of the fittest", that's the way the economic world operates. It's a survival jungle out there. And it's not just in a capitalistic society where big business appears to have no heart. It's true in every society, even those who claim communism and socialism level the field for everyone. They don't. And it's because of human depravity. Unless God changes the heart, sin and self-centeredness and greed control it. The result: the focus is on receiving, rather than giving.

God has a better plan. His Church's philosophy is caring for and helping the weakest. That makes giving the most important. Our world desperately needs this change of attitude. And the Church needs to lead the way.

The evangelical church takes seriously its' charge to give the hope of salvation to the world. That's commendable. All gifts pale in comparison with the gift of eternal life. Unfortunately, we have been accused of emphasizing this while neglecting the physical and material needs of people. Is this criticism valid? Perhaps, to some degree. However, a recent study by Syracuse University professor Arthur Brooks indicates otherwise. His findings were published in November, 2006, with the title, "Who Really Cares; The Surprising Truth About Compassionate Conservatism". What he found was that the "Religious Right" are more generous givers, in every way, than religious liberals and non-religious people. And this includes everything from monetary contributions to volunteering time to donating blood. He found that regular church-attenders give four times more money per year than those who attend only occasionally or never. While much of that giving is through the church, they also give more to secular charities. Furthermore, they are more likely to ""behave in compassionate ways towards strangers." (Source: Christianity Today, February, 2007.)

While the report is encouraging, we need to ask ourselves if we are doing all God expects of us. Ladies have long known that often the way to a man's heart is through his stomach. Missionaries have found that approach is effective in reaching people who are spiritually lost. Ministering to physical and material needs may open the door to a spiritual ministry.

Following the Scriptural pattern of giving requires both kinds. Almsgiving was practiced in Bible times. The Mosaic Law of the Old Testament instructed God's people to leave some of their harvest for "the alien, the fatherless, and the widow". (Deuteronomy 24:19-22) King Solomon took the requirement a step further: "If your enemy is hungry, give him food to eat; if he is thirsty, give him water to drink." (Proverbs 25:21) Jesus gave His approval to the giving of alms when He instructed that it be done with pure motives. In the Sermon on the Mount, He said, "When you give to the needy, do not let your left hand know what your right hand is doing, so that your giving may be in secret. Then your Father. . . will reward you." (Matthew 6:3)

Our Lord is the best authority for the principle of giving. While one of His statements somehow failed to get recorded in the Gospels, the Apostle Paul quoted it, and Luke recorded it, in Acts 20:35: ". . . It is more blessed to give than to receive." There you have it! We stand on solid ground when living by this principle.

Why Give?

Do you ever feel bombarded by requests for you to contribute to some Cause? Sometimes it seems almost every day brings a new solicitation by phone or mail or in person. Solicited giving has always been a part of life. Modern technology has just made it more convenient and complex. And more obnoxious. Sometime we say yes and sometimes we say no. We decide what's most important. That's necessary, because it's impossible to give to every appeal. This represents the lowest form of giving.

A second type of giving is clearly need-based. It's a response to difficult circumstances or tragedy. And it is a higher form of giving. It comes from the heart, even if it is with some reluctance.

A third form of giving comes with a spirit of caring. And it's the highest kind. It causes people to give their money, time, and energy in hurricane disaster relief. It sends them into the inner city to minister to hurting humanity. It motivates them to go half-way around the world to share with people very unlike themselves. It helps them reach out to a suffering neighbor.

We don't have to look beyond the life of Christ to find a reason for giving. His whole life was about giving. He gave hope to the hopeless, healing to the diseased, sight to the blind, comfort to the afflicted, acceptance to the rejected, new birth to the spiritually dead, the promise of eternal life to the dying. Why should we give? Because *it's Christ-like.* And we should follow His example. It's true; we can't be Christ-like without giving. The nameless boy who shared his lunch caught that spirit. And Jesus multiplied it so it fed thousands! He'll multiply the impact of our gifts, too.

If you need another reason, consider the benefit for you; *it makes you a better person.* There is a life-cleansing effect on the giver. Some self-centeredness is washed away. Prejudice barriers are broken down; horizons are broadened. There is an emotional phenomenon called "helpers' high". It refers to the personal benefit received through volunteer service. And there is a similar benefit that comes from heartfelt giving. It could be called "givers' high". An emotional blessing does warm the heart of the sincere giver.

If a body of water has no outlet, it becomes stagnant. But if the inflow is matched by outflow, there's freshness and vibrant life.

Our lives need outflow, also , or they become stagnant. Archbishop
Desmond Tutu pointed out that God's arithmetic is different. When
you subtract by giving away, you get more. Jesus expressed this
truth, also, when He said: "Give, and it will be given to you. A
good measure, pressed down, shaken together and running over, will
be poured into your lap. . ." (Luke 6:38) The benefit may not be
monetary, but it is very real. While it's not the motivation for giving,
it is the result.

I have great memories of some special Christmas Eves. Many
years ago, my wife and I started a tradition of inviting someone to our
home for dinner; someone who, otherwise, would be home alone.
Sometimes it was a university student who was unable to go home for
the holiday; sometimes a member or family in the congregation. I'm
sure our blessing was at least equal to theirs. In fact, I enjoyed it so
much that, after my wife passed away, I continued the practice, even
though my cooking skills were not the greatest. (As far as I know, no
one became ill!)

Giving is important because *it makes the world a better place.*
The need is just as great, now, as when Jesus was on earth. The
motivation for giving reaches far beyond the blessing received by
the giver. And the results go beyond our present generation. Noah
Benshea, author of the inspirational Jacob the Baker book series,
advised, "Do not kiss your children so they will kiss you back, but so

they will kiss their children." Selfless giving impacts the world with a powerful influence. It tends to be contagious. It can even trigger an epidemic of giving.

We give because *God has so generously given to us.* "God so loved that He gave." It has been said that "you can give without loving, but you can't love without giving." God loved us enough to send Jesus to the cross to die for our sins. That's giving at the highest level. It's beyond our ability to understand or duplicate. But we can follow His example. Jesus told His disciples, and us, "Freely you have received; freely give." (Matthew 10:8) While much of the giving that occurs at Christmas doesn't have a spiritual motivation, it's appropriate to the season. People celebrate the world's greatest gift by generously giving to others. More unselfish giving occurs during the Christmas season than any other time in the year. Maybe there's still a bit of God's image in human nature, after all!

What Should We Give?

It's not enough to simply "give". Something specific must be given. Something more than the traditional Christmas gifts. Something more than gifts to special people on special occasions. Something more valuable than anything you can buy in the finest department store. In the Sermon on the Mount (Matthew 5 and 6), Jesus provided a good list. We'll consider a few of them here. You may look for others in the passage.

Mercy: that's a needed gift. Some need it more than others, but everyone needs it sometime. A lady was complaining to the photographer about her portrait. Her complaint: "It just doesn't do me justice!" After looking at the picture and then at the customer, the brave photographer commented: "Ma'am, what you need isn't justice; you need mercy." Jesus said, "Blessed are the merciful." Have you extended mercy to anyone lately? Perhaps it's needed by a family member or a neighbor or a co-worker or a homeless person who crosses your path.

Peace: that's needed, too. It's not just nations that are at war. Serious conflicts rage in homes, communities, work places, even churches. Peacemakers can make a difference. It can be risky business. But God has called us to be risk-takers for a worthwhile cause. Give the gift of peace. If there is to be "peace on earth", it has to begin in someone's heart. And it must be expressed in human relationships. According to an ancient Chinese philosophy, there's a chain reaction: "If there is righteousness in the heart, there will be beauty in the character. If there is beauty in the character, there will be harmony in the home. If there is harmony in the home, there will be order in the nation. When there is order in the nation, there will be peace in the world." Perhaps that philosophy is overly optimistic on a world scale, but it works on a personal level.

Reconciliation: a special kind of peace-making. It means being the one to take the first step to peaceably resolve a difference with someone. Matthew 5:23-24 indicates this needs to be done before "offering our gifts at the altar". Worship of God is empty of meaning if our hearts are filled with animosity toward our "brother". It's better to give a piece of your heart than a piece of your mind! Many years ago, while attending a wedding in a Roman Catholic church, I noticed a door with this name-plate: "Reconciliation Room". Perhaps every church needs a room like that.

Light: the antidote to darkness. The Bible has many references to the spiritual darkness of the world. (See Luke 1:79, Acts 26:18, Colossians 1:13, I Peter 2:9) Jesus came proclaiming, "I am the light of the world. Whoever follows me will never walk in darkness, but will have the light of life." (John 8:12) And He didn't stop there; He told His disciples, "You are the light of the world." (Matthew 5:14) An awesome responsibility for them – and for us! We can give light to our world only as Jesus' light is burning within us.

The story is told of Robert Louis Stevenson, as a small child, looking out his bedroom window as dusk turned to night. He was watching a lamplighter move along the street lighting the lamps. When asked what he was doing, he replied, "I'm watching a man punch holes in the darkness." That's our mission: to "punch holes" in the spiritual darkness of our world; to bring light to those lost in sin's night. We're called to light up our world. That's a gift worth giving.

How to Give

In Matthew 6:1-4, Jesus tells us to give quietly and humbly. No trumpet fanfare, please! There's a story of an old man who carried an oilcan with him wherever he went. Whenever he encountered a squeaky gate or door, he quieted it with a few drops of oil. It was his gift to those who would follow him. He expected and received no reward, except for the inner warmth of giving his gift. That's giving, as God intended it to be.

For 26 years, a man known only as "Secret Santa" roamed the streets of Kansas City every December, quietly giving people money. In the first years he gave 5 and 10 dollar gifts. He kept increasing the amount until, in recent years, he was giving $100 bills. For all those years, his identity was a secret. But we now know his name. In November, 2006, a 58-year-old businessman from the Kansas City suburb of Lee's Summit, Missouri, revealed that he was the mysterious giver. Terminally ill with cancer and weak from chemotherapy, Larry Stewart decided it was time to go public with his intense belief in the value of random, secret acts of kindness. He did it with the hope that others would be inspired to follow his example.

Christ-like giving requires *the giving of oneself with the gift*. And that means a greater sacrifice. It comes from the heart, not just the purse. Usually, it's an investment of time and energy. It's often said that if you give a man a fish, you feed him for a day, but if you teach him to fish, you feed him for a lifetime. That's a good principle. It has a practical application to the mechanics of giving. And it's another way of saying we need to give ourselves with our gifts. It takes time and energy to "teach a man to fish".

Somewhere, I read a story about a young boy on a mission field who brought a beautiful shell and presented it to the missionary. She realized he had walked a half-day to bring his gift, and she gently scolded him for making such a long trip. He smiled and replied, "Long walk part of the gift."

Give without expecting something in return. Real giving is not merely an exchange of gifts. This is not a criticism of gift exchanges; rather, it's a challenge to do more than give to those who give to us. There's something beautiful about anonymous giving. It's what made the generosity of Kansas City's "Secret Santa" so special. Most of us don't have the resources to duplicate his actions. But all of us need to sometimes give to someone who can't or won't respond with a gift. It's good for the soul!

In II Corinthians 9:7, we're admonished *to give cheerfully*. No long faces. No clenched teeth. As Paul stated it, we should not do it "reluctantly or under compulsion". A man reported he was told to pay his taxes with a smile. So he tried it. But it didn't work; the government wanted cash. But God is impressed by your smiley face – if it comes from a cheerful and giving heart. According to Paul, "God loves a cheerful giver." Okay, He loves the tight-fisted Scrooge, too. But the cheerless giver misses out on the rich blessings of giving generously and joyfully.

God's plan for giving is best – for both giver and receiver. Only then is it true that "You're more blessed in giving than in receiving."

Applying the Principle – Discussion Questions

1. What makes Christian giving distinctive?

2. What did Jesus mean by "giving in His name"?

3. Is giving worthwhile without love? . . . without sacrifice?

4. Is it possible to give too much? Under what circumstances?

5. How should Christians respond to panhandlers and homeless people?

6. What did Paul mean by "excelling in the grace of giving"? (II Cor. 8:7)

7. How do you reconcile Jesus' teachings on giving with Paul's statement: "If a man won't work, he shall not eat"?

CHAPTER 6

LIFE'S BEST INVESTMENTS AREN'T LISTED ON THE S AND P 500

Imagine yourself a spectator at the New York Stock Exchange. The opening bell sounds and the frenzied trading begins. The atmosphere is hectic, almost chaotic, as buyers and sellers make their transactions. In offices far away, analysts study the market trends and prepare their analysis. Around the world, financial advisors guide their clients in investments. Meanwhile, individual investors track the progress of their 401 K's, IRA's, stocks, bonds, and a host of other options. Government encourages investments with tax deferrals, shelters, and write-offs. Banks add to the variety of choices with savings accounts, certificates of deposit, money market funds.

Then there's the strange terminology used in the financial world: bull market, bear market, dollar cost averaging, mutual funds, junk bonds, spyders, cubes, diamonds – the list goes on and on. Pretty confusing, isn't it? How do you know where to invest? Welcome to investment terminology jungle!

We can understand the feelings of one perplexed investor. After talking with his financial advisor, he commented to his neighbor: "First he said my assets were frozen, then liquidated, and now they seem to have evaporated." The stock market is volatile. Real estate value rises and falls. The value of collections depends on the whims of prospective buyers. All earthly investments have inherent risk. A good reason for making some investments that will bear dividends for eternity!

In material terms, we're simply discussing ways to make your money work for you. And this isn't wrong, if it's done with integrity. After all, we should provide for future needs. Security is a legitimate goal. So, what's the problem? There's a built-in danger: the process of investing can easily infect our values. The benign desire for money may become malignant. Our possessions are prone to possess us. Treasures can become tyrants.

There's an old joke about a leopard that was killed by a hunter. His pelt was made into a beautiful fur coat. Sometime later, two of his leopard friends saw it in a store window, priced at $10,000 dollars. One remarked to the other, "You know, he was a lot better off before he was worth so much." Likewise, we may become "worse off" if we become "better off".

Jesus' Investment Warnings

In the book, <u>The Parables He Told</u>, David Redding wrote: ". . .when a rich man comes to the question, as every American must, 'What shall I do with my money?', Jesus marked it: 'Handle with extreme care.' We say, 'Watch, so it won't slip through your fingers.' He branded it radioactive and cried, 'Beware lest it eat into your soul.'"

Does this mean investing for gain reveals greediness? Is the profit motivation sinful? Is a capitalistic economy un-Christlike? Well, what did Jesus say about it? Much of what He said on the subject was in His parables. In Matthew 13:44-46, He seemed to approve of reaching for something better, as He told the stories of men spending all they possessed to buy a hidden treasure and a very valuable pearl. Also, He gave the familiar parable of the talents, in which He clearly commended investing. (See Matthew 25:14-27)

On the negative side, in Luke 12:16-21, our Lord told the parable of a rich man who was a fool because he was investing in bigger barns. So, what would Jesus say to us today? The Stock Exchange didn't exist when He walked the streets of Jerusalem. The Bull and Bear Markets were unknown. He didn't advise His followers on Capernaum Co-op investments. But He gave some powerful words of caution and advice for all: "Do not store up for yourselves treasures on earth, where moth and rust destroy, and where thieves break in and steal. But store up for yourselves treasures in heaven, where moth and rust do not destroy, and where thieves do not break in and steal. For where your treasure is, there your heart will be also." (Matthew 6:19-21) That's just as relevant now as when He spoke those words. Here's the key issue: what treasure has your heart? The "rich fool's" problem wasn't his bigger barns; it was wrong treasure in his heart. In Matthew 6:24, Jesus drew a line in the sand: "You cannot serve both God and money."

Investment Strategies

When I was young, I read that a fundamental principle of banking was "have fun with the interest but don't touch the principal". If that was true, it meant merely maintaining the status quo. Today, the emphasis is on investing for gain. And that means not using the interest for "fun" but re-investing it to gain compound interest. Just a few days ago, I heard a financial guru state that if a young person invested only $3 a day and allowed it to compound with interest throughout his lifetime, he would become a millionaire. That boggles my mind! Whether or not that statement is totally accurate, it is true that we must *invest for the long-term.*

Our investments should include something that will pay dividends now and that will outlast this life. An old man was observed planting a peach tree. The spectator teased him, saying, "you won't live long enough to eat fruit from that tree." He smiled and replied, "That's alright; all my life I've been eating peaches from trees someone else planted." That's the investment spirit God desires for all of us. That's concern for the right kind of "legacy".

Probably you're familiar with the terms "bull market" and "bear market". Here's a simple definition: a bull market means investing with the expectation that market prices will rise; a bear market means selling with the expectation that prices will decrease. I believe the *Christian life should be a "bull market"*. After all, Proverbs 4:18 says, "The path of the righteous is like the first gleam of dawn, shining ever brighter till the full light of day." The one who is getting the most out of this life is also investing for eternity. Our goal is providing for future needs. Security is the primary objective. And security in eternity is far more important than material prosperity here. Jesus recommended a better buy than "blue chip" stock --- eternal gold! Best of all, the dividends accrue both in this life and in eternity.

One day, as a funeral procession passed through an intersection, a Brinks armored truck turned from the side street and followed the motorcade of mourners. Someone on the sidewalk was heard to mutter: "Who says you can't take it with you?" *While it's true "you can't take it with you", you can send something on ahead.* As Dave Brannon **w**rote in an <u>Our Daily Bread </u>devotional, "There's good news and bad news if wealth is what you want. The good news is God's Word does promise riches to the believer. The bad news is that it doesn't have anything to do with money." But that's okay with the genuine Christian; he's looking for riches beyond this world.

Jesus' words indicate our investments in this life determine the riches awaiting us in heaven. Remember how interest compounds? Well, God has an even better compounding formula! And the growth will continue throughout eternity. True, the return won't be in dollars or pesos or euros or any other form of money. Those won't be needed in heaven. Our riches will be something far greater.

Balancing the Temporal and the Eternal

Consider the variety of material investors. It's not just about stocks, bonds or real estate. There are the "collectors". It might be stamps or coins or art or anything that is interesting and has potential for increase in value. There are the "showmen" (and women) who gather valuable items to impress others. Their motto: "diamonds are forever". Their primary gain is their satisfaction in having something better than others. Then, there are the "precious metal people". They believe gold, silver and other valuable metals are the best investments. Finally, there are the "land-grabbers" whose goal is to accumulate vast real estate holdings. But all these things must be left behind when this life ends.

For the Christian, the only real "estate" is in heaven. We depend on Jesus' promise to prepare a place for us. We look forward to the wonderful things awaiting us in heaven, knowing heaven will be far greater than the description in Revelation 21. So we make our investments with eternity in mind.

Here's a Christian formula for balancing the temporal and the eternal: *1. Remember God still owns your property, even though you hold the title. 2. Hold earthly possessions and collections loosely.* That formula enabled Job to survive the loss of almost everything and still say: "The Lord gave and the Lord has taken away; may the name of the Lord be praised." (Job 1:21) It worked for him; it will work for you.

In contrast to Job, we have the New Testament story of the Rich Young Ruler. (Matthew 19:16 – 24) He had done well with his earthly investments. He was wealthy. But He was unhappy. He knew he was a spiritual pauper. He had no eternal possessions. So, he came to Jesus with this plaintive plea: "what must I do to get eternal life?" Our Lord's answer was startling: "go sell your possessions and give to the poor, and you will have treasure in heaven." A radical remedy! However, it sounds like Jesus was offering him a deal: buy your way into heaven with good works. But there was one more stipulation: "Then come, follow me." He knows how to balance the temporal and the eternal. *Just follow Jesus!* Sadly, the young man was unwilling to accept the terms. He left with an empty heart, eternally destitute.

As Christians, we're citizens of God's Kingdom on earth. So we need to be investors in it. In the Old Testament, tithing was the "law of the land". And Jesus gave His support to tithing our income. But the tithe is not a mere "temple tax" to fund the operation of the Church. I believe it's God's way of helping us make some investments for eternity. It's one way of "sending something on ahead".

God usually doesn't require a vow of poverty for citizenship in His Kingdom. But He does demand the *willingness to surrender* to Him all we possess. That's the essence of complete consecration. He has a way of pin-pointing our heart treasure. He asks: "May I have that? Will you let me invest it, for you, in eternal treasure?"

Investment Options

Money isn't the only form of Kingdom investment. Diversify; that's one of the basic rules of financial investing. And it will multiply your eternal returns. Jesus called His fisherman disciples to become "fishers of men". *To follow him is to invest in ministry.* We're called to be ambassadors, not spectators. Participants, not just recipients. I once heard Dr. Bob Moorehead, pastor of a megachurch in Spokane, Washington, tell of a phone call he received from a lady who had just moved to his city. She asked what his church had to offer for her and her Christian family. He responded by asking what she had to offer to the church. Then, without waiting for her answer, he added, "we can offer whatever you have to offer as a Christian." A bold but truthful answer!

Dr. D. James Kennedy once stated, "The most destructive

heresy that has ever plagued the church is the idea that the ministry of Jesus Christ is to be performed by professional clergymen and not by the entire body of Christ." Remember: the new birth experience includes a ministry assignment.

The word "talent" has changed in primary meaning since Jesus used it in the well-known parable. (See Matthew 25:14-30) Then, it was a unit of money. Now, it generally refers to a person's abilities. And we interpret the parable with that definition. Interestingly, the only condemnation was to the one-talent man – not for having only one talent, but for burying instead of investing it. A long time ago, someone quipped, "It's not what you'd do if great riches should e'er be your lot; it's what you are doing with that dollar and a quarter you've got." The lesson for us: *invest, don't bury.* It's irrelevant whether we rate as a "one" or a "ten". Whether it's currency or capability, the purpose of investing is increase. And talents tend to become greater through use.

God's Word challenges us to *invest in people.* In Ephesians 6, Paul writes about the priority of family relationships. In I Timothy 5, he tells us how the caring spirit should prevail in the church family. James 5:19 tells us to reach out to the "wandering brother". In Luke 10, Jesus told the parable of the Good Samaritan to teach reaching out to neighbors. In Matthew 10:42, He said giving a cup of water is a good investment.

Investing in people can be risky. It's often disappointing. In this life, you may not see a good return on your investment. But it's God's will. So it's a good venture. It's worth the risk. Remember, someone (probably many) invested in you. Perhaps your family comes to mind. It wasn't just your cost in dollars; there was sacrifice of love, tears, and prayers. A mother reported that one day she asked her small son if he liked the new perfume she was wearing. He replied, "Oh, Mommy, I like you better when you're kitchen-flavored." It does cost something to be "kitchen-flavored".

You may not have been privileged to grow up in a Godly home. But someone made an investment in you. A popular young Peace Corps volunteer was leaving for home, after completing his assignment. An, old, toothless native woman poked him in the chest and said, "When I'm with you, I like me best." I assume she meant he made her feel good about herself. You may never serve in the Peace Corps, but you can help someone gain a new sense of self worth. Do it with the love of Christ, and you have made an eternal investment in people.

Here's the final segment of this discussion: *you need to invest in yourself*. God created you in His image. He endowed you with great potential. And He planned for you to become better than you are. Your challenge: become the person He designed you to be.

That means you must believe in yourself. Push yourself beyond your comfort zone. Like Paul, leave the past behind and "press on toward the goal to win the prize for which God has called (you) heavenward in Christ Jesus." (Philippians 3:14) Will you always reach all your goals? No. But, as Bud Robinson once said, "It's better to shoot at the moon and miss than to shoot at a skunk and hit."

I'm not advocating a mere self-improvement project. You can't do it alone. Rather, it's a joint venture with God. A partnership. You do your part and He will do His. The sculptor Michelangelo once saw a stained, misshapen, discarded piece of marble in a builder's yard. Pointing to the unattractive stone, he requested, "Let me have it. I'll take it to my studio. An angel is imprisoned in that marble and I must set it free." God sees something special in you. He wants to "set it free". And, with your cooperation, He will.

Sound investing requires wise choices. True materially. And especially true spiritually. The world's best investments – whether stocks, bonds, gold, real estate, or any valuable collection – all pale in comparison with a portfolio that pays dividends for eternity. As martyred missionary Jim Elliot wrote, "He is no fool who gives up what he cannot keep in return for what he cannot lose."

Applying the Principle – Discussion Questions

1. What can we do, as Christians, to make capitalism more Christlike?

2. Does our desire for security conflict with trusting God?

3. What are signs that we're too concerned about material things?

4. What can we do to control the desire for material things?

5. What kind of legacy would you like to leave behind when this life is over?

6. What is the difference between talents and "spiritual gifts"?

7. What does Paul mean by "godliness with contentment is great gain"? (I Timothy 6:6)

CHAPTER 7

YOU CAN'T REALLY SERVE WITHOUT A SERVANT HEART

Several months ago I was notified that I was a winner in a drawing. Amazing! I hadn't even entered. But I didn't win a new car or lots of cash. I was chosen to serve on a jury. I have to admit I wasn't real excited. And it wasn't a convenient time. But I did my civic duty and appeared at the jury selection room at the appointed time. But was I really ready to serve, or was I just going through the motions?

Jury duty isn't the only form of serving. For example, consider a Marine on duty in Iraq, a restaurant waitress, and the pastor of a church. What do they have in common? All are servants. The Marine is serving his country; the waitress is serving her customers (she is called a "server"); the pastor is serving his congregation and his Lord. These are just a few examples of self-giving. Servanthood is good. Not something usually aspired to, but good.

Our principle includes two key words: *serve* and *servant.* The dictionary definitions are interesting; *servant:* "one who serves others"; *serve:* "to be a servant". Sounds like we're going in circles! Surely we can reach a better understanding than that. Well, consider this: both words come from a Latin word meaning "to be a slave". Therefore, serving is no light matter. It's serious business. Especially for those who profess to be followers of the Servant Savior. Following Him means our service is transformed into ministry.

Jesus pulled no punches when He talked about serving. We're destined for servitude. In Matthew 6:24, He said someone or something will be our master: "No one can serve two masters. . . You cannot serve both God and money." This suggests the only alternative to serving God is being a slave to materialism, selfishness, and worldliness. We have a clear choice. Both include service, but what a contrast! Not only does God richly reward His servants (see Matthew 6:25-34), but, in serving God, we serve others. So, the blessings of service are multiplied.

In Matthew 20:28, Jesus stated His life purpose. It was twofold. He came to die for the sins of the world. He came to save. But He also came to serve. And, in verses 26 – 28, He told His followers to follow Him in humble service. Then, as John 13:2-17, tells us, He demonstrated it by washing His disciples' feet; a timeless example of self-giving love. It's desperately needed in the home, the real proving ground of the Christian Faith. Often inhibitions are low and demands are high. As someone has quipped: "Man is an unreasonable creature who wants a home atmosphere in a hotel and hotel treatment at home." In contrast, the late Dr. Mendell Taylor once told of a busy housewife who was asked how she could keep washing dishes that won't stay washed, making beds that won't stay made, sweeping floors that won't stay swept, and changing babies that won't stay changed. She replied, "I'm not just washing dishes or sweeping floors or making beds; I'm building a home in which God can reveal Himself." She had caught the spirit of the Master Servant!

A spirit of serving is much needed in the church. In Galatians 6:10, Paul writes: "Therefore, as we have opportunity, let us do good to all people, especially to those who belong to the family of believers." When the mother of James and John asked Jesus to give them special honor in His kingdom, His reply was a gentle rebuke: "whoever wants to become great among you must be your servant. . ." (Matthew 20:26) What a tragedy if we fail to follow our Lord's instructions in the place where we worship Him! The world wants to know how the gospel works in life's closest relationships. And certainly the church is a place where we rub shoulders with our fellow Christians, many of whom are all too human. Many years ago, an unknown poet with a wry sense of humor wrote:

"To dwell above with folks we love

Oh, yes, that will be glory.

To dwell below with folks we know,

Well, that's another story!"

The Apostle Paul was under no illusions about conflict in

the church. He had sharp disagreements with some fellow leaders, including Peter and Barnabas. Yet, he wrote to the church of his day, and to us, ". . . serve one another in love." (Galatians 5:13) He knew loving service would be a unifying force.

The world in which we live needs people who want to serve. Our nation stopped the practice of human slavery nearly 150 years ago. Professional "servants" have become rare. But the need for people who serve is as great as ever. Local communities give special honor to the rare individuals who give of themselves in outstanding service. We, as Christians, need to ask ourselves if we are serving our world as we should.

Service Activities

Consider the many areas of serving: elected or appointed officials are referred to as public servants; people, like me, serve as jurors in court trials; employees receive recognition for "service years". We have service clubs, military service, repair service, pastoral service, restaurant servers, plus a host of other ways of serving. Natural disasters bring a response of sacrificial service as people generously give of their time and energy to help those in need. Both the church and society provide many opportunities for volunteers. Early retirement, plus better health in old age, makes it possible for many to give more time in response to these challenges. As Dr. Elton Trueblood stated, "For the Christian, retirement is liberation for Christian service."

While these service activities are good and beneficial,

sometimes they fail the "serious business" test. They may be performed half-heartedly or even for selfish reasons. A deeper level is needed.

A Heart for Service

"His heart just wasn't in it" – that's a common explanation for someone's lack of success. It applies to serving, also. Whether your activity is vocational, avocational, or recreational, you won't be effective if "your heart isn't in it." A word of caution: success isn't always apparent. Sometimes you may have unjustified feelings of failure. But, as columnist Ann Landers once wrote, "If you can face your God and say 'I have done my best', then you are a success." Let God balance the books when He sees best. Even if it's not 'till eternity.

Have you ever felt slapped in the face when you did a good deed? It happens. Too frequently, it seems. And it can quickly cool your enthusiasm. A heart for service keeps you going when the going gets rough.

History tells of a famous Greek general, named Epaminondas. After giving many years of outstanding service to his country, he was demoted when some of his enemies gained power. He was even humiliated by being made a garbage collector. His response: "As the position will not bring honor to me, I will bring honor to the position." And people said his village had never been kept so clean as during his term of duty. That's a heart for service! It's where real serving originates. It's how it continues.

Two New Testament ladies named Mary and Martha had different ways of ministering to Jesus. One day He was relaxing with them in Martha's house. Probably their brother, Lazarus, was there, too. We don't know what he was doing, but we know about Martha's activities. She was bustling about in the kitchen, preparing dinner. She wanted it to be special. Jesus was their guest! And she was frustrated. Mary wasn't helping one bit. Just sitting in rapt attention at the Master's feet. It was just too much for Martha. She exploded, "Lord, tell her to help me!"

Most people are pretty hard on Martha. Luke's account (Luke 10:38-42) portrays her as the poster girl of misdirected service. Jesus' response seems to agree. In a loose paraphrase, it would sound like this: "Mary, it doesn't matter if the lamb chops aren't perfect, the vegetables get mushy, and the cake resembles a flat tire. There are more important things than a perfect dinner." But His words did not constitute a reprimand. His saying "Martha, Martha" tells us that. Rather, it was gentle instruction to a friend. He recognized both ladies had a heart for service. Martha expressed it through hospitality; Mary revealed it through undivided attention. I'm not even convinced Jesus was saying one was more important than the other. Each was using her special gift. Both were serving with their own unique strength. That's both sensible and Biblical. So don't be so hard on Martha!

It's possible (perhaps even common) to become so preoccupied with performing the service that we lose sight of its' purpose. That was Martha's mistake. It wasn't that she was the mistress of the kitchen; the kitchen was mastering her. It kept her from serving Jesus the way her heart really desired. This well-known Bible story tells us one very important truth: service without relationship misses the mark. It's true, whether you're serving Jesus or a neighbor or a co-worker or a fellow believer.

How about the rewards? There's a silly joke about a man who was awarded a medal for being the most humble one around. But it was taken away from him because he wore it. The one with a genuine heart for service doesn't have that problem. He or she is not seeking rewards or medals. Some time ago, a group of food service workers urged the passage of a law that would require restaurants to add a 20% gratuity to every customer's bill. This was the topic of conversation on a radio talk show, recently, when a waitress called to express her opinion. In stating her opposition to the campaign, she said: "I believe if I give good service, good tips will come. I'm doing just fine without this law." What a refreshing attitude! It's not that she doesn't like receiving tips. She's human. She has bills to pay.

But, for her, service outweighs reward.

The Servant Heart

There's a still deeper dimension for us to consider. While a heart for service may be emotion-based, a servant heart is a condition of the spirit. And it should be present in every follower of Jesus. In Philippians 2:5-7, Paul wrote, "Your attitude should be the same as that of Christ Jesus. . . who. . . made Himself nothing, taking the very nature of a servant." That's an awesome responsibility! And we can fulfill it only when controlled by His spirit within us. Service is then transformed into ministry.

Recently, in my home church, two immigrant ladies shared their experiences of serving in a new and humbling way. One is from Korea; the other from South America. Both had socially respected positions in their native countries. Both are now working as custodians at Olivet Nazarene University. After wrestling with the normal human emotions, each accepted her new role as an opportunity for ministry to college students. And two new servant hearts were born.

Each of us has received so much from others: from our Lord and from our peers. As someone has pointed out, God doesn't comfort us just to make us comfortable, but to make us comforters, also. Only when we have grasped this truth can we say we have a servant heart.

What is a Servant Heart?

It is, first of all, *Christlikeness.* It beats with His passion for ministry. An old hymn-prayer, written by Judson W. VanDeventer, expressed the craving of a servant heart: "Give me a love that knows no ill; give me the grace to do thy will. Pardon and cleanse this soul of mine. Give me a heart like thine." That prayer echoes in the heart that really cares about others. And it's the result of the change God makes within.

The servant heart has *a greater desire to serve than to be served.* That's contrary to human nature. Sometimes it's nice to be served. Suppose you are going out for a meal. If you're in a hurry, you'll go for fast food. If you are especially hungry, you might choose an all-you-can-eat buffet. But if you want to relax and enjoy yourself, probably you'll go to a sit-down restaurant. Your server will bring your menu, take your order, serve your food, refill your drink, and clear your empty plates. All you have to do is enjoy your meal. Pretty nice! And it's not wrong to enjoy being served. But the servant heart has a higher calling. It looks for opportunities to be the servant instead of the served. It knows we serve God by serving others.

Someone has defined compassion as "your pain in my heart". The servant heart has a similar quality; *it has a willingness to be vulnerable.* It goes beyond a caring spirit; it risks hurt for the sake of ministry. And the risk is real. Father Damien was a Belgian missionary who served a leper colony in the Hawaiian Islands. He was the only healthy man among 600 horribly diseased bodies. After many years of service there, one day something happened that transformed his ministry. As he was pouring boiling water into a pan, some of it splashed onto his bare foot. But he felt no pain. Suddenly, it dawned upon him; one of the symptoms of leprosy is the inability to feel pain. He had contracted the disease. He ran to the church and rang the bell. As his poor worshippers gathered, he strode to the pulpit, spread his arms, and greeted them: "Fellow lepers, Fellow lepers!" Sometimes the servant experiences painful emotional injury, also. But it's worth it. As someone has observed, when we stand before our Maker, He'll be impressed by our scars, not our medals. The "crown" awaiting us in not for wearing; it's for casting at Jesus' feet.

What the Servant Heart Does

It *motivates to active ministry.* It pumps energizing blood to hands that reach out to the least, the lost, and the lonely. . . to feet that climb over obstacles to walk on dusty paths of humble service. . . to the tongue that articulates words of encouragement, comfort, and faith to someone battered by life's storms. It prays, like Saint Francis of Assisi:

"Lord, make me an instrument of thy peace.

Where there is hatred, let me sow love;

Where there is injury, pardon;

Where there is doubt, faith;

Where there is despair. hope;

Where there is sadness, joy."

The love of God is beyond our comprehension. But the servant heart *gives a glimpse of God's love* in life's daily routine. In Our Daily Bread, writer Dennis De Haan tells of a cleaning lady who had worked 40 years in the same building. A reporter asked how she was able to stand the monotony. She replied: "I don't get bored. I use cleaning materials that God made. I clean objects that belong to people God made, and I make life more comfortable for them. My mop is the hand of God."

God has called us to a life of holiness. (See Romans 12:1; II Corinthians 7:1; I Peter 1:15; II Peter 3:11; Hebrews 12:14) The servant heart *puts holiness into action*. There's a story about a travel group in the Far East. Pointing to a cave in the side of the mountain, the guide said, "A holy man lived there his entire life. Food and water were brought to him, but no one was allowed to ever see him. He was one of the great holy men of our history." A member of the travel group muttered: "So what?" A skeptical world is more impressed by holiness in action than by holiness in seclusion. And that's one great reason we need servant hearts!

Applying the Principle – Discussion Questions

1. What are some service opportunities within the church?

2. What service should Christians give within their communities?

3. How do you know if you are spending too much time and energy in service?

4. What are signs of wrong motivation in service?

5. What is the difference between service and ministry?

6. Is public praise for outstanding service good or bad? Why?

7. What should you do if the service you are giving seems unappreciated or becomes burdensome, and you begin to feel it's not worth the effort?

CHAPTER 8

GOD'S SCHOOL OF PRAYER HAS NO ALUMNI

Graduation. That's the normal goal of education. Get that diploma, "sheepskin", degree. It's a mark of achievement. Especially if you graduate with honors. It prepares you for life in the "real world". Helps you land a job. Pretty important to help pay off those astronomical school bills!

Alumni are important people to their alma mater – for a variety of reasons. I know; I'm a graduate of three educational institutions. (Guess I was a slow learner!) There was good old Auburn High. Every few years I receive an invitation to come back for a class reunion. Then, there's Olivet Nazarene University. Every year they have Homecoming. Of course, I'm invited. Now I'm considered a "Golden Grad". Maybe I'm supposed to increase my financial contribution, now that I have such status. There's also Nazarene Theological Seminary. It seems I'm a popular graduate of theirs, too. Probably for the same reasons.

God has a school, too. It's the School of Prayer. If you're a follower of Jesus, you're enrolled. It's a different kind of school;

there are no graduates! You're expected to be perpetually enrolled.
No special honors are conferred. No one graduates *cum laude, magna cum laude, or summa cum laude.* You receive no diploma to frame
and hang on your wall. That would be impressive. But God knows
better. The absence of graduation is for your benefit, as well as His
Kingdom. The learning should never stop.

The Mysteries of Prayer

One of life's great mysteries is prayer. Humans engage in it
because of an innate faith in a higher power; because of awareness
of needs; because of desperate circumstances. But most of us don't
really understand how prayer works. It's beyond our comprehension.
We know prayer is our means of contact with our Creator. But we
don't fathom just how that communication occurs.

In a cartoon, "The Family Circus", written by Bil Keane, little
Billy says to his mother: "I wrote down a prayer. Does God have
a fax machine?" At least, in his simple faith, Billy had an idea how
God might receive his prayer; I don't have a clue! There are billions
of humans on this earth. Potentially, there could be millions praying
at the same time. How does God handle that many prayers? I don't
know.

We who live in this age of amazing technology do have
an advantage over our ancestors. We talk on our phones that
are connected to tiny optical fibers that transmit thousands of

conversations simultaneously. We send millions of E-mail messages, at the same time, around the world via the internet. We watch television broadcasts that are sent to satellites in space, then sent back to our living rooms. If human minds can create such marvels of communication, surely the Infinite God can hear our prayers.

Probably our greater concern is the mystery of God's answers to our prayers. Why doesn't He answer as we expect? After all, Jesus said, "ask and it will be given you, seek and you will find, knock and the door will be opened to you. For everyone who asks receives. . ." (Matthew 7:7 – 8) Sounds pretty clear cut. But the fact is, God doesn't always answer in the affirmative. And His answer may not come on our timetable. It might come as a "no". Or He might say, "wait a while." And sometimes we can't hear His answer. So, how do we cope with this mystery? We must believe, in our hearts, that our Heavenly Father knows best. Also, we must remember God answers from His perspective of eternity, which is much different from our experience of time.

There are many reasons for the answers He gives. Here's one to remember. God answers our prayers with a "yes" often enough so we keep praying, but not so often that we take His "yes" for granted. He knows it's not good for us to acquire an entitlement mentality. Don't expect God to be a permissive parent or a celestial

Santa Claus who can't say "no".

Rabbi Harold Kushner once said, "I don't like the notion that when we pray and don't get answers, God has considered our request and said 'no'. I don't know much about the nature of God. But I know prayer makes life better and richer for me." Remember this: delay doesn't necessarily mean denial; God may have a better plan. In Luke 11:1, Jesus' disciples made this request: "Lord, teach us to pray." Sometimes the disappointing answers to our prayer requests are simply lessons in our continuing education. And learning those lessons does make life "better and richer".

Prayer helps us get to know God in a growing personal relationship. We learn to trust Him when we don't understand. It's a paradox that, through praying, we resolve its' mysteries. Furthermore, by continuing in God's School of Prayer, we become better equipped to cope with the other perplexities of life. And that's without even graduating!

The Purpose of Praying

A man was overheard praying: "Oh, Lord, if you'll get me out of this jam, I'll never bother you again!" Sadly, that story reflects the purpose of too much praying: to get out of some "jam". God intends prayer to be something more than last resort desperation; more than a self-centered wish list; more than shallow requests for superficial desires.

Toward the end of his life, author C. S. Lewis said he was

fortunate God hadn't granted all the silly requests he had made. Ouch! Most of us can say "amen" to that. But God is patient with us. The Psalmist had prayed some prayers that were worse than silly. Yet, in Psalm 6:9, he declared: ". . . the Lord accepts my prayer." And His acceptance extends to you and me. That's important; acceptance is a more basic need than approval.

Some of our prayers must be confusing even to God. The mother of legendary football coach Paul "Bear" Bryant did not approve of his football career and never attended the games he played in or coached. He liked to tell the story of her prayer: "Dear God, keep him from playing, but if he does, let him win."

The most fundamental purpose of prayer is communication between the Heavenly Father and His children. He didn't create us to be spiritual orphans or forgotten children. As the Psalmist declares, "The Lord is near to all who call on Him. . ." (Psalm 145:18) James 4:8 adds, "Come near to God and He will come near to you." He desires communion as well as communication with us. Sincere prayer brings that desired closeness and intimacy. He's waiting for us to come to Him. Before we present our requests, we need to present ourselves. We need fellowship with Him even more than we need his intervention in our lives.

Communion with God is food for the soul. A young mother confided to her pastor that she felt weak and defeated spiritually.

When he asked her about her devotional life, she became defensive. "You don't know what it's like to have three crying children all pulling at you at the same time. Most of the day is a madhouse. I admit I often go several days without time to read my Bible or pray." The pastor smiled and asked, "How often do you feed your baby?" She replied, "every four hours, and one feeding around 3:00 a.m." "Don't you find it hard to get up and feed him in the night, and sometimes wouldn't you like to just skip the daytime feedings?" the minister probed. Then he suggested, "Maybe you could just give him three or four bottles one day, then let him wait a few days for the next feeding." After a brief moment, the startled mother responded: "Okay, I get it. If I fed my baby like I'm feeding my soul, he wouldn't be very healthy."

In a <u>Reflecting God</u> devotional, Joan M. Wilson tells of someone testifying, "I want to know Him so well and communicate with Him so regularly, that when I pass into eternity, I will be able to greet him with, 'As I was saying, Lord. . .'." Prayer should not be a mere religious ritual but comfortable communication with our God. He's not so big that He doesn't care about the details of our lives. Remember, Jesus taught us to speak to Him as "Our Father. . ." That's a special relationship!

A second purpose of prayer is forgiveness and cleansing. It's the means by which we receive the benefits of Jesus' sacrificial death.

A small girl spilled some fruit juice on her pretty dress in Sunday School class. She told her teacher, "Don't worry; Mom can get it out with Pray and Wash." Actually, she had the right combination for getting rid of the stain of sin. I John 1:9 says, "If we confess our sin, He (God) is faithful and just and will forgive us our sins and purify us from all unrighteousness." Since God is the one who does the forgiving, the confession is made to Him – through prayer. Titus 2:5 tells us, ". . . He saved us through the washing of rebirth and renewal by the Holy Spirit. . ." So there you have it – "Pray and Wash".

There's an old hymn, written by Robert Lowry, that asks the question, "What can wash away my sin?" That's the sinner's desperate question. The next word in the hymn is "nothing". – That's the hopeless answer of the world. It has no solution for the sin problem. But the verse of the hymn follows with another phrase: ". . . but the blood of Jesus." That's God's answer. And it's our hope.

In presenting Jesus as the Great High Priest, the writer of the epistle to the Hebrews contrasts the inadequacy of the Old Testament animal sacrifices with His sacrificial death. His conclusion: "How much more, then, will the blood of Christ, who through the eternal Spirit offered himself unblemished to God, cleanse our consciences from acts that lead to death, so that we may serve the living God!" (Hebrews 9:14) And that cleansing is experienced through the miracle of prayer and faith.

Another purpose of prayer is to harmonize our will with God's will. He created us with a physical brain. It has an awesome capacity for intelligence if functioning properly. He has given us the power of free will. He expects us to use it. That's a vital part of His image in us. But there should not be a "battle of the wills". For spiritual victory, we must surrender our will to His will – if they are in conflict. It will change us for the better. Then we can pray "in the Spirit".

An unknown Confederate soldier reportedly penned the following beautiful testimony:

"I asked God for strength, that I might achieve;

I was made weak, that I might learn humbly to obey.

I asked for health, that I might do greater things;

I was given infirmity, that I might do better things.

I asked for riches, that I might be happy;

I was given poverty, that I might be wise.

I asked for power, that I might have the praise of men;

I was given weakness, that I might feel the need of God.

I asked for all things, that I might enjoy life;

I was given life, that I might enjoy all things.

I got nothing that I asked for – but everything I had hoped for.

Almost despite myself, my unspoken prayers were answered.

I am, among men, most richly blessed."

Too often we pray for what we think will make our lives more comfortable and pleasant. Perhaps we should be praying, first of all, for strength equal to our circumstances.

I would suggest one more purpose of prayer: *to release some of God's power to do what He already wants to do for us.* I've already admitted my lack of understanding of some of the prayer mysteries. And that's true of this one. But it is evident God has imposed some limitations on Himself in giving us free wills. This is another example of His dependence on our response.

Here's a strong Biblical support for stating this purpose. In Joel 2:28, the prophet spoke for God: "And afterward, I will pour out my Spirit on all people. Your sons and daughters will prophesy, your old men will dream dreams, your young men will see visions." Now, fast forward several hundred years to the Day of Pentecost. When Peter preached to the crowd after the historic outpouring, he declared, "This is what was spoken by the prophet Joel. . ." (Acts 2:16) God had promised. Jesus reminded His followers of the promise, along with a command for them to wait in Jerusalem for its' fulfillment. (Acts 1:4) So we know God wanted to do it. But it didn't happen until obedient disciples prayed in the upper room until they were "with one accord". (Acts 2:1 KJV) And we humans are still involved, today, in releasing God's power through prayer.

An awesome responsibility!

The Power of Prayer

Prayer is the continuing education of the soul. It must never stop. There's an old saying "practice makes perfect". Well, we can never become perfect in prayer. But there is a *practice factor* in effective praying. And it is powerful. The word "practice" means something people do to improve performance – as in music or athletics. No matter how talented they may be, those who excel can never stop practicing. The word also may refer to something one does regularly, as an occupation or life work. Physicians are described as being in "medical practice". In this sense, every Christian needs to be in 'prayer practice".

In I Thessalonians 5:17, the Apostle Paul admonishes us to "pray continually". (NIV) Other translations are: "pray without ceasing" (KJV), "never give up praying" (Goodspeed), and "always keep on praying" (Living Bible). Obviously, Paul didn't mean we have to actually pray all the time. Probably it means for us to be in a continual spirit of prayer. And certainly it means we should never give up our lifetime "prayer practice".

There is *value in habitual praying:* grace at mealtime, family and personal devotions, bedtime prayers. I once saw a cartoon depicting a small boy coming out of church and saying to the pastor, "I do most of my praying in pajamas." I'm sure God's heart is touched by a child's "Now I lay me down to sleep" prayer. And an adult's sincere, simple prayer pleases Him, even if it is a habit. As someone has said, "God hears more than our words; He listens to our hearts."

General prayers may have some benefit, but *focused praying* connects God's power with the need. Don't overlook *the focus factor.* We need to be specific and passionate. The prayer closet is no place for apathy! Consider what a magnifying glass can do with the warm rays of the sun. When they are focused to a small point, the resulting intense heat can start a fire. Too much of our praying is a shotgun approach – shooting at a variety of needs, hoping to hit something. But there's little intensity in our prayer. And we wonder why there no positive results.

James 5:16 instructs us: "The effective, fervent prayer of a righteous man avails much." (NKJV) Fervency brings focus to our requests. And God is moved by our fervor. The effectiveness of prayer doesn't depend on its length or audible volume, but on its earnestness and focus.

In May, 2003, mountaineer Aron Ralston escaped death, after being pinned under a large boulder 6 days in a remote mountain canyon. With the hope of being rescued fading, he somehow found the strength and courage to cut off his forearm with his pocket knife. He then managed to walk several miles before someone found him. After his recovery, he reflected on his amazing survival: "I may never fully understand the spiritual aspects of what I experienced, but I will try. The source of the power I felt was the thoughts and prayers of many people, most of whom I will never know." It was a miracle of focused prayer, including people who didn't even know him. It was anonymous intercession focusing God's love and mercy.

How can you explain the strength of united prayer? Consider the way a cable is made, by twisting or braiding smaller wires together to multiply their strength. Somehow, our individual prayers join together with other similarly focused prayers to increase the impact. We do know Jesus indicated there is strength in numbers. For example, in Matthew 18:19-20, He said: "I tell you that if two of you on earth agree about anything you ask for, it will be done for you by my Father in heaven. For where two or three come together in my name, there am I with them."

Spiritual life comes from God's power, not our puny strength – whether it's individual or group. And prayer is *the power line of the soul.* Keeping the power connection intact is crucial. We can't afford to become disconnected. The world, the flesh, and the devil try to get us unplugged. And then there's corrosion. It's a problem in electrical connections. It's a bigger problem for many Christians. Too busy to pray. Too much desire for things. Infected by the spirit of the world. Unconfessed sin. And spiritual corrosion breaks our power connection.

But we can keep connected. Galatians 5:25 says, "Since we live by the Spirit, let us keep in step with the Spirit." That's the secret of keeping the power current flowing in us. God matches His power to our needs and our capacity. The electric utility company uses transformers to reduce the 72,000 volts in its high tension lines to the power level needed in our homes. God has a "spiritual transformer" – the Holy Spirit. As we continue in His School of Prayer, He will provide the right power for our needs.

So don't try to graduate; concentrate on being a good student of prayer!

Applying the Principle – Discussion Questions

1. What is the most important lesson you have learned in God's School of Prayer?

2. What should we do when we can't determine God's answer to our prayer?

3. What helps us avoid having an "entitlement mentality" in our prayer life?

4. What do you think the psalmist meant when he stated "the Lord accepts my prayer"?

5. What helps you sense you are actually communing with

God when you pray?

6. It is obvious prayer should not be a battle of our will against God's will. But how do you know if there is a conflict?

7. What helps you pray with focus and intensity?

CHAPTER 9

FORGIVING IS BETTER THAN FORGETTING

Have you ever heard someone exclaim, "I can forgive him, but I can't forget it?" Maybe you've even said it yourself. The implication is that forgiveness isn't enough. Something more is needed. It suggests forgetting is a step beyond. Therefore, better. Not true! In case you question our principle, let's do a simple, side by side comparison:

Forgetting is a human weakness. Forgiving is spiritual strength.

Forgetting is mental. Forgiving is spiritual.

Forgetting is normal human activity. Forgiving is Godlike.

Forgetting is involuntary. Forgiving is voluntary.

Forgetting may be temporary. Forgiving is permanent.

Forgetting erases good and bad memories. Forgiving prevents bitter memories.

Forgiving Heals the Forgiver

It's beyond debate that our world would be better if there were more forgiveness. Less family squabbles, divorces, road rage, lawsuits, murders. For individuals, there would be less resentment,

retaliation, remorse; more peace, harmony, serenity. Jesus made

forgiveness a cornerstone of the Christian Faith. But its importance

goes far beyond; it's a major lubricant of social interaction. It's also a

healing oil for the human spirit.

A woman refused to take the tranquilizing medication

prescribed by her doctor, saying, "the last time I took it I found

myself being friendly to people I wouldn't even speak to otherwise."

Sounds like she really needed those tranquilizers! God didn't design

us to be unforgiving. Our bodies do not function well when stressed

by destructive feelings such as anger, resentment, and bitterness.

Since we're not equipped with emotional exhaust pipes, the disposal

must occur within. Otherwise, those "fumes" accumulate inside us.

And they can attack physical organs of the body --- even vital ones.

Many scientists feel they can sometimes cause death.

Many years ago, an interesting experiment with a cat revealed

how stress affects the body. The digestive system of the animal

was observed through a fluoroscope in a laboratory as he purred

contentedly. His food was being processed efficiently. Then, the

door opened and a huge dog bounded into the room. Immediately,

the cat's back arched; his fur rose; his eyes dilated. But the most

significant reaction occurred inside. The digestive process slowed,

then stopped altogether. The lesson for us: if resentment affects cats so adversely, it's also destructive in human bodies.

Jesus recommended a stress-reliever that's better than a physical relief valve; it's called "forgiveness". While it may seem contradictory to self-interest to let go of perceived injustices, we never really recover until we forgive. Wild animals are known to become dangerous when they have unhealed wounds that fester. And the outward violence of humans usually is the expression of a malignant spirit. Forgiveness may be withheld because of a desire to "get even". But that's a psychological impossibility. Frequently, people say they need "closure", when what they are seeking is revenge. Contrary to the old adage, revenge is not sweet. It's sour, bitter, and destructive. It imprisons us. Conversely, freedom comes through forgiveness. It stops the endless cycle of negative reaction.

A significant part of life consists of reaction to actions of others. And forgiveness is a healing reaction. Especially for the forgiver. So stop singing that "somebody done me wrong" song and start forgiving! It's good for your soul.

Forgiving is Christ-like

Jesus spoke as the Savior, not as a psychologist. It's true much of what He said about forgiveness involved our relationship with God. His forgiveness of our sins – that's the greatest human need. But it's also essential in human relationships. So important that, in Matthew 6:14-15, He made it a requirement for our receiving God's forgiveness.

"The Lord's Prayer" is our pattern prayer. In it, Jesus taught us to pray with forgiveness in our hearts. "Forgive us our debts as we have forgiven our debtors." (Matthew 6:12) Luke's version is slightly different: "Forgive us our sins, for we also forgive everyone who sins against us." (Luke 11:4) In Luke 6:37, He makes this requirement even more clear: "Forgive and you shall be forgiven." Mark 11:25 says, ". . . if you hold anything against anyone, forgive him, so that your Father in heaven may forgive you your sins."

What do these Scriptures mean? Is this a forgiveness trade? Are we making a deal with God? No. Jesus is telling us what is necessary to remove the blockage to our receiving God's forgiveness. And He's telling us the words" forgiven" and "forgiving" are like the proverbial love and marriage; you can't have one without the other.

A man called his bank when he discovered his account had been mistakenly charged with a withdrawal. The bank employee couldn't resist pointing out a previous incident when an error had occurred in the customer's favor without a complaint being made. To which the man replied: "That's true, and I could forgive one mistake, but not two!" Jesus taught forgiveness that goes far beyond two. When Simon Peter asked how many times he should forgive someone, Jesus replied, "seventy times seven." (Matthew 18:21-22) That's a lot of forgiving! Actually, it means an infinite number. No limits.

There's a story that when Leonardo Da Vinci was painting "The Last Supper", he became very angry with an acquaintance, even to the point of threatening him. When he returned to work on the painting, he could not finish the face of Jesus. So much anger and resentment was raging inside him. Only when he made the decision to forgive did he find the inner peace necessary to complete the face of the Prince of Peace.

Jesus didn't just teach forgiveness; He personified it. He put His preaching into practice. He practiced it when His family judged Him mentally incompetent. . . when deeply disappointed by deserting disciples. . . when agonizing alone in Gethsemane while His Inner Circle slept. . . when wounded by the stinging betrayal of His friend Judas Iscariot. . . when suffering under Calvary's crushing weight of the world's sins. He experienced the full range of our emotional hurts – plus more. And, so, He was able to pray "Father, forgive them. . . " (Luke 23:34) -- because He already had.

There's an unusual old gravestone in a cemetery near New York City. There's no name, date of birth or death; nothing to identify the deceased. Just one word: "Forgiven". What a powerful, wonderful word! Especially when it means our eternal salvation. But human forgiveness is pretty awesome, too. A long time ago, someone wrote, "to err is human; to forgive is divine." That's true; the act of forgiving reflects divinity. It's a super-natural reaction.

Sometimes forgiveness doesn't come easily. We live in a strange world. Some unsaved people are nicer by nature than some Christians are by grace. And that can make it difficult when we're faced with the need of forgiving a fellow believer. It helps to remember the new birth experience doesn't de-humanize us. Faults persist. Growth in grace requires time. But God's requirement doesn't make exceptions. And Jesus gave us the example of forgiving the worst of human failures.

Forgiving is Active, not Reactive

In an article titled "The Unnatural Act", Philip Yancy wrote, "In the final analysis, forgiveness is an act of faith. By forgiving another, I am simply trusting that God is a better justice-maker than I am. By forgiving, I leave issues of fairness for God to work out. I defer to Him the scales of justice. Wrong does not disappear when I forgive. But it loses its grip on me and is taken over by God. He knows what to do." (Christianity Today, 4-8-91, pp. 36-39)

Unless it's a shallow act, forgiveness is costly. It involves an honest examination of our inner being. Our attitude and reactions are reviewed. It requires frankly facing the facts of what happened and why. It doesn't mean "sweeping something under the rug" and pretending it never happened. Often, it takes some time to deal with the hurt, let go of the anger, and release the sad event to God.

Here's the best definition of forgiveness I've ever heard: "It's surrendering my right to hurt you for hurting me." With that surrender, a miracle occurs. There's a healing within the heart of the forgiver. The process may be costly, but it's curative. The relationship may not be healed, but there will be peace in the surrendered heart. And, more often than not, there will be a softening in the heart of the forgiven one.

Our Principle states "forgiveness is better than forgetting." Apparently Jesus would agree; He had a lot to say about forgiveness, but not much about forgetting. The Apostle Paul wrote about forgetting the past and reaching toward what is ahead. (Philippians 3:13) But sometimes you can't forget. And sometimes you shouldn't forget. Without memories, we don't learn from the past. And, as someone has said, "those who fail to learn from the past are doomed to repeat it." God gave us memory for a purpose. Forgiving doesn't remove bad memories; it removes the bitter aftertaste. Remembering our own mistakes may help us forgive someone who has hurt us. So don't be too concerned about forgetting!

Forgiving Begins at Home

Tragically, the most difficult challenge for many is self-forgiveness. They may have found the grace to forgive others but find it much harder to forgive themselves. This emotional victory needs to be won, for it lays the foundation for all healthy forgiveness.

Begin with the confidence that God created you. He made you in His own moral image. In His sight, you are of infinite worth. But He also made you human. That means you have imperfections, faults, limitations. Before you can achieve self-forgiveness, you must have self-acceptance. That doesn't mean you ignore your short-comings. It doesn't mean settling for being less than the best you can be. But it does require tuning out the voices that would rob you of belief in yourself.

Several comic strips thrive on humorous put-downs. For example, there's Peanuts, in which Lucy is the merciless tormentor of poor Charley Brown. Then, there's Jon, in Garfield. He's the victim of continual abuse by his fat cat. Another is The Born Loser. Thornapple is frequently humiliated by his heartless boss. We're amused by the antics of these fictional characters. But it's painful when it happens to us. And most of us have had similar experiences. It's no fun to be cut down to size. . . to have our balloon burst. . . to be the recipient of "the perfect squelch".

It seems there's always some "Lucy" around to put you down or line you up or chew you out. Don't listen to her (or him). Remember your self-worth isn't dependent on anyone else's opinion of you.

God doesn't create junk. Rather, He made you a spiritual "lump of clay". He wants to shape your life into something beautiful. So the third step in self-forgiveness is to place yourself on His great potter's wheel and allow Him to mould you into His planned design. Self-surrender is the doorway into self-forgiveness. You are a work of God in progress. That awareness can liberate you from the prison of self-blame.

Forgiving others begins in the home. Family relationships especially need the healing ointment of forgiveness. It's the place where we are most likely to "be ourselves". Faults become more evident. Social inhibitions vanish. Tempers may turn into tantrums. In one home, a small child had just spilled some grape juice on the new, light-colored carpet. The mother was very upset and let loose a barrage of angry words. Later, she apologized: "It was an accident; I'm sorry I yelled at you. Please forgive me." With an innocent smile, the boy replied, "it's okay, Mommy. I love you when you're good and when you're bad."

You've just read a beautiful little story. It's packed with so much meaning. It reminds us that an apology often starts the process of forgiveness. In the home, and in all human relationships. Someone has to start it.

Many years ago, the Burma Shave Company advertised its

product with a catchy series of little signs along major highways. Here's one I remember:

The saddest words

Are these that rhyme.

If he won't dim his,

I won't dim mine.

This little limerick points out a major roadblock on the forgiveness highway. Someone has to make the first move. Usually it involves an apology. That's humbling. But it's also heart-melting. Even if it doesn't change the heart of the other person, it does something in the forgiver – if it is genuine.

Currently, there's an internet website, "Project Forgiveness. com". It's a place for non-confrontational apologies and requests for forgiveness. An anonymous person recently placed this one: "Papa, I'm sorry I broke curfew again. Please forgive me." Well, at least it's a start. However, the anonymity of the request makes its sincerity rather suspect. Modern technology can do amazing things, but I'm not sure it can achieve forgiveness. It has to be a heart to heart event!

Back to our Principle: Don't worry about the forgetting; just focus on forgiving.

Applying the Principle – Discussion Questions

1. What does forgiveness mean to you?

2. What is the relationship between Christ's commands to forgive and to not judge?

3. What are some reasons for the difficulty people have in forgiving?

4. Should our forgiveness of others have "conditions" attached to it?

5. Need we forgive someone who doesn't ask for forgiveness?

6. Why is "getting even" a psychological impossibility?

7. Is it harder to forgive fellow Christians than unsaved people? If so, why?

CHAPTER 10

GENUINE LOVE MAKES A SOLO COMMITMENT

Genuine love isn't dependent on a relationship. Sounds a
bit heretical, I'll admit. But it's the foundation of the principle I'm
proposing. The key word is "genuine". It's natural to desire a loving
response. Everyone needs to be loved. But real love is more about giving
than receiving. It comes from the heart, not just the emotions. It's given
without strings attached. The attitude is not "I love you – *because*"; it's "I
love you – *regardless*".

Many years ago it might have been appropriate to say, "I can't
give you anything but love." Since we now live in such an affluent but
self-centered society, perhaps the words should be changed to "I can give
you everything but love." But material gifts are a poor substitute for
love. It is presence, not presents, that is most needed. Giving of ourselves
in love means caring, sharing, risking, and being vulnerable. And our
mission of loving isn't complete until the other person senses our love.

Love is expressed in relationships. Someone has described it
as the universal language. Created in God's image, with the capacity
to love and be loved, we're unique. Animals may have devotion to
their masters or their mates, but they cannot love as humans can.

Tragically, that gift has been perverted in ways God never intended. The Greek language has at least three words for love – *eros* (sensual love), *phileo* (friendship love), and *agape* (God-generated love). But English has only one, and it is used for everything from "puppy love" infatuation, to the sex act, to product preference, to the love of God. We need to determine the meaning of love – from God's perspective.

Defining Love

A long time ago, someone described love as "many-splendored". That's both poetic and perceptive. But it's also a classic understatement! It's hard to find an adequate definition. In the words of an old television commercial, "Love comes in all sizes."

Children have some interesting ideas about love. Greg, age 8, wrote: "love is the most important thing in the world. But baseball is pretty good, too." Floyd, age 9, said, "love is foolish, but I still might try it sometime." David, age 8, shared his experience: "Love will find you, even if you are trying to hide from it. I've been trying hide from it since I was 5, but the girls keep finding me." Regina, age 10, gave her perspective: "I'm not rushing into love. I'm finding fourth grade hard enough."

Adult definitions are inadequate, too. What appears to be love often is something much less. A pastor was quite impressed by the visible affection of an older couple in his congregation. Frequently, he observed them holding hands. One day he commented he thought it was wonderful they were still so much in love. The wife responded, "Reverend, it's not about love. It's just the only way I can keep him from cracking his knuckles."

Actually, holding hands can be a good expression of physical affection. There's something beautiful about an elderly couple holding hands as they journey through life. But real love is something much deeper than an act or an emotion. Photographer James Van Der Zee showed a youthful picture of his wife to a friend, with this comment: "When she was young I loved her because she was beautiful. When she became old I loved her because I knew her." That's real love for a lifetime!

Here's a general definition of love, according to the dictionary: "Strong affection based on admiration or desire; self-giving loyal concern that freely accepts another and seeks his or her good." That's a fairly comprehensive definition, but it's pretty vague. Here's a picturesque definition that's much better: "Love is two hearts tugging at one load." That's a beautiful description – of an ideal situation. But many situations are far from ideal. Since we can't control anyone else's love life, we must focus on our own. Therefore, we need our principle: "genuine love makes a *solo* commitment."

We can have – and practice – love even when there's no loving response. But it must be more than physical attraction . . . feeling or emotion . . . a state of the mind. . . sexual desire. . . automatic

Christian grace.

The Apostle Paul gave us the best definition in the Love Chapter (I Corinthians 13). In it, he used the Greek word *agape*, so he was speaking of "God-generated love". First, he tells us what love is not, then he defines it in terms of its characteristics. It is not superhuman, but it has the additive of God's grace. It covers all kinds of relationships: parent/child, husband/wife, family members, friendships, church family, "neighbor", romance. Paul's list of love qualities is profoundly practical: patience, kindness, absence of envy, not boastful or rude, not self-centered, not easily angered, doesn't hold a grudge.

An unknown writer has expressed similar truth in real life terms. Love is:

> Slow to suspect – quick to trust.
>
> Slow to condemn – quick to justify.
>
> Slow to offend – quick to defend.
>
> Slow to expose – quick to shield.
>
> Slow to reprimand – quick to forbear.
>
> Slow to belittle – quick to appreciate.
>
> Slow to demand – quick to give.
>
> Slow to provoke – quick to conciliate.
>
> Slow to hinder – quick to help.
>
> Slow to resent – quick to forgive.

The deepest love comes from a love relationship with God. Loving Him gives both motivation and ability to love others from the heart. I John 4:7 says ". . . love comes from God." Then, in verse 16, John adds, "God <u>is</u> love. Whoever lives in love lives in God." This is the kind of love Paul describes in I Corinthians 13:7-8 (Phillips paraphrase): "Love knows no limit to its endurance, no end to its trust, no fading of its hope; it can outlast anything. It is, in fact, the one thing that still stands when all else has fallen."

The Love Decision

"Falling in love" sounds so much more romantic than "deciding to love". And it may be an appropriate description of emotional love. When the "love bug" bites, strange things happen. But even this kind of love requires decisions. For example, before a man proposes marriage to a woman, he decides to do it. Then he decides how and where to do it. And the woman decides whether or not to accept the proposal. (Probably she had already decided before he "popped the question"!) Actually, we don't "fall in love"; we plunge into love -- by decision. Even if it's only an unconscious choice.

Genuine love of God requires decision, also. It's not something that happens just because our emotions are stirred. It is faith-based, but it's also an act of the will. And that element is crucial when we don't understand the difficult circumstances of our lives. Sometimes we're tempted to feel God has let us down. The decision enables us to keep on loving Him, regardless. And it helps to remember He continues to love us when we actually do let Him down!

Human love is an emotion. It's influenced by physical characteristics, actions, response, and circumstances. It's vulnerable to change. Decision brings stability to changing emotions. The intensity of the romance or the closeness of the friendship may subside, but decision preserves the vital part of the love.

You can count on it; love relationships will test the depth of love. The test may come through personality differences. There's an old story about a wife who angrily chased her husband out the door with a broom, then cried because he left without kissing her goodbye. Men, on the other hand, are notoriously unobservant of details that are important to women. Many a husband has bought a gown or dress for his wife because he could "just see her in it", when she had been wearing one just like it for years.

The test may come through change in the other person. It could be physical, mental, or even spiritual. Our bodies tend to change in shape over the years. Usually resulting in a lower center of gravity. Advancing years may bring decreased mental capacity or physical disability. Life circumstances can cause disagreements or misunderstandings. Without a solid decision to love, the emotion of love may die.

Deciding to love means taking the initiative. And there is a risk of rejection. But it's worth the risk. Motivational speaker Zig Ziglar told a story of a small boy who became angry with his mother. He ran out of the house toward a hillside screaming "I hate you!" Hearing the echo of his voice, he ran back home and told his mother there was a mean boy shouting that he hated him. The wise mother said, "Just go out there again and shout 'I love you!'" Sure enough, the boy heard the love echo. And it's likely you will, too.

The Love Commitment

Commitment gives permanence to decision. Keeps us from changing our minds, falling out of love, or letting it die from neglect. It's a determination to make love last for a lifetime. It puts I Corinthians 13 into action. It works at keeping love growing and maturing. It practices "loving in spite of"; not just "because of". Love in return for love is a natural reaction; love in return for rejection is a super-natural commitment.

Many Scriptures indicate *agape* love comes from a changed heart. Colossians 1:5 speaks of "love that springs from within". Galatians 5:22 describes it as "the fruit of the Spirit". "We love because (God) first loved us," according to I John 1:19. But loving the way we should doesn't happen automatically just because we're

Christians.

There are far more Scriptures that command us to love. We're told to love our God, one another, our neighbors, our spouse, even our enemies. We're commanded to pursue love, to "put on" love as a breastplate, to serve one another in love. All these require human volition. Without commitment, love is shallow or short-lived.

A graduate student, studying cello under the great cellist Pablo Casals, performed a number, for his teacher, with technical precision. Expecting praise, the student was shocked by Casals' criticism: "You're playing the notes, but not the music." Likewise, love may produce mere notes, without any real melody.

Genuine love commitment creates the music in relationships. It transforms love's performance into an unending symphony. It harmonizes the notes. Establishes the tempo. Adjusts the volume. Communicates a strong message of a promising tomorrow. Warms the heart. Brightens the horizon. Builds bridges over canyons of misunderstandings. Tempers strength into gentleness. Renews hope. Enhances faith. Preserves lasting love. When the Apostle Paul declared love is the greatest, he surely must have meant love with commitment!

Remember our principle: genuine love makes a *solo* commitment. The commitment holds, whatever the other person does. It requires being patient with faults, affirming, submitting, putting the other person first. The practical realities of life reveal

its depth. Several years ago, the "For Better or Worse" comic strip

depicted the mother and daughter shopping for valentines. The girl

asks, "Mom, who makes up all these valentines?" The mother replies,

"Someone who works at the greeting card company. They have lots

of writers who think up hundreds of ways to say 'I love you'." The

daughter's second question: "Mom, do they mean it?" A good

question – for all of us!

The Love Connection

In The Four Loves, C. S. Lewis wrote, "Love anyone and your

heart will be wrung and possibly broken. If you want to make sure

of keeping it intact, you must give it to no one. . . To love is to be

vulnerable." But if you subtract the willingness to sacrifice, you're left

with only hollow emotion. Sacrifice is the quality that makes our love

most Christ-like.

Love in the heart needs expression in the life. And it occurs

where our life path intersects with someone else's road. Even God's

love had to find expression in His relationship with His creation.

"God is love" may satisfy the theologians, but most of us need the

assurance that "God so loved the world that He gave. . ." (John 3:16)

That's the starting point of love in relationship.

Follow the Scriptural trail of sacrificial love. It begins with

God's love for us in that best-known verse from John's Gospel. It tells us of God's greatest gift to the world: "For God so loved the world that He gave *His one and only Son. . .*"

The trail continues as John tells us of Jesus' command: "Love each other as I have loved you. . ." (John 15:12) Later, John tells us the significance of the command: "This is how we know what love is: Jesus Christ laid down his life for us, and we ought to lay down our lives for our brothers." (I John 3:16)

In John 15:13, our Lord described this as the ultimate expression of sacrificial love: "Greater love has no one than this; that he lay down his life for his friends."

But the trail doesn't end at the house of a friend. Jesus didn't limit the command to loving nice people. He even instructed us: "Love your enemies and pray for those who persecute you. . ." (Matthew 5:44) It's a fact that not everyone is naturally loveable. But He made no exceptions. Sacrificial love is a solo commitment.

Not every act of heroic self-sacrifice is an expression of sacrificial love. Many are simply the result of a developing tragedy, uncommon courage, and a rush of adrenaline. Situations calling for the sacrifice of life are rare, but love frequently requires personal sacrifice. In the home. At the workplace. Among neighbors. With fellow believers. Wherever there are people. I John 3:18 challenges us: "Dear children, let us not love with words or tongue, but with actions and in truth."

A few days ago, I was deeply touched by a caller on a radio talk show. She was the mother of a Down syndrome child, who also had a serious heart defect. When the host asked how she and her husband were coping with having this handicapped child, she replied: "We keep asking ourselves how can we love better; how can we sacrifice more." That's sacrificial love in action! And that's a true "love connection".

Applying the Principle – Discussion Questions

1. Can you love someone if you don't like him or her?

2. What does it mean to "love with all your heart"?

3. Of the following words, which is the most opposite of love: dislike, hate, reject, scorn?

4. What have you found to be the hardest test of love in human relationships?

5. What should you do when your love is rejected?

6. Is it possible to "fall out of" real love?

7. What is the greatest expression of human love you've ever witnessed?

CHAPTER 11

THE CALENDAR DOESN'T TELL YOUR REAL AGE

You have a birth date. It pinpoints the time you began your individual presence in this world. It's the official record that you exist. You must have it for a host of legal transactions. Just try to obtain a Social Security card, driver's license, bank account, loan, or a passport without one! It's very specific. It doesn't allow you to say "I was born in 1954, give or take a few years." You might joke about being "39 and holding", but the calendar doesn't lie. You're getting older, whether you admit it or not. And that aging process brings change.

Someone jokingly listed six stages of a man's life: six months, all lungs; five years, all ears; fourteen years, all feet; twenty-one years, all muscle; forty-five years, all paunch; sixty years, all in. Obviously, that's an oversimplification of life's journey. We don't all fit neatly into those six categories. Some are never "all in", as long as there's breath in their body. Contrary to what the calendar says, real age is relative. Some are "old" at 30, while others are "young" at 80.

It's a strange paradox that most people want to live long, but few want to become old. Actually, real age is more a state of the mind than a condition of the body; more an inner attitude than outer muscle. I remember a parishioner who had a double hernia surgery when he was 90 years old. When I visited him in the hospital, he referred to his 65 or 70 year old roommate as "the old gentleman". My 90 year old friend wasn't really old, because he was still young at heart.

You can't change your official birth date. So, the calendar doesn't lie. But here's our paradoxical principle: it doesn't tell your real age. You determine that by the way you deal with the aging process. Admittedly, that's not easy – whatever your age. The young are told to "grow up", and they have a natural desire to become older. On the other hand, older people are admonished to "age gracefully". That's a tall order! We'd like to hold back the hands of the clock. We'd like to re-capture "our get up and go that got up and went".

Someone recently circulated the following bit of verse on the Internet:

"I look in the mirror, and what do I see?

A strange looking person who cannot be me.

For I am much younger, not nearly so fat

As the face in the mirror that I'm looking at.

Oh, where are the mirrors that I used to know,

Like the ones of thirty years or so ago?

All things have changed, and I'm sure you'll agree:

Mirrors are not as good as they used to be!

Sometimes we use the phrase "the prime of life". When is this ideal time in life? Is it 20, 30, 40, or 50? Someone has suggested 40 is the old age of youth, while 50 is the youth of old age. There is no magic moment -- or year – that defines the peak in your life experience. You are not "over the hill" just because you've passed some perceived change point in time.

Time is divided into three periods: past, present, and future. But yesterday blends into today, and today blends into tomorrow. So, really, today is the first day of the rest of your life. I would suggest you consider today your prime of life – whatever your age. Don't waste today on yesterday or tomorrow. Many squander today by dreaming of a day that's forever past or fantasizing about a future that may never come. A common mistake of aging is expending more energy looking back longingly than looking forward expectantly.

In The New Republic, Stanley Kauffman asked, "What is memory?" He answered the question: "It's not a storehouse, not a trunk in the attic, but an instrument that constantly refines the past into a narrative, accessible and acceptable to oneself." This is true as long as we don't try to live in the past. There's a big difference between memory and journey. We create problems when we try to make thoughts of the past a repeat journey instead of a completed event. Today is the prime of life because it puts yesterday into perspective and lays tomorrow's foundation.

Healthy Aging

"Healthy aging" is commonly associated with maintaining a healthy body. Exercise regularly. Eat a balanced diet. Avoid junk foods. Get adequate sleep and rest. Practice moderation. Control your weight. Extend your life through positive lifestyle choices. That is good advice. But, no matter how well we treat them, our physical bodies won't last forever. In <u>AARP Magazine</u>, Dr. Andrew Weil wrote, "I consider the fixation on anti-aging and life extension to be a distraction from the important goal of healthy aging."

There's an interesting scientific term that relates to aging: *compression of morbidity.* It means limiting life's end period of disability and dependency to as short a span as possible. The goal is to have a long, healthy life that ends quickly without a long struggle with the death process. And that's a worthwhile goal. It's not wrong to try to preserve good physical health. God expects us to take good care of our bodies. But healthy aging is not just physical.

Good health is more than a strong, robust body. Our minds need maintenance, also. And most of the advice listed above can help promote good mental health. Although we may be guilty of neglecting its' care, most of us would agree it's even more important than physical health. A senior citizen with a good sense of humor wrote: "I can live with my arthritis, my dentures are just fine. I like my new bifocals, but, oh, how I miss my mind!"

Age does affect our thinking ability. Brain cells die. The good news is that, recently, scientists have concluded that brain cells can be regenerated through good mental exercise and right attitudes. The Apostle Paul was a step ahead of those scientists when he wrote: "Finally, brothers, whatever is true, whatever is noble, whatever is right, whatever is pure, whatever is lovely, whatever is admirable – if anything is excellent or praiseworthy – think about such things." (Philippians 4:8) Our world is filled with mental garbage; we can't afford to let it pollute our thought processes.

Near the end of his "love chapter", Paul wrote of the difference age makes in one's thought life (I Corinthians 13:11). Every age brings different temptations. Self-pity is one that plagues those in advanced years. It can incarcerate us in a prison of hopelessness. A railroad employee accidentally locked himself in a refrigerated boxcar. When he was unable to attract anyone's attention by pounding on the door, he eventually gave up hope of being rescued. As he felt his body numbing with cold, he began writing on the wall: "I'm becoming colder. . . I can hardly write. . . these may be my last words." When the boxcar was finally opened, he was found, still and cold in death. And yet the temperature inside was 56 degrees. The refrigeration unit had been out of order for months.

There was no physical reason for his death. He was a victim of his hopeless attitude. While the loss of hope may not cause our death, it is a sign of unhealthy aging.

Spiritual health is most important of all. For every age group. And it should not deteriorate with advancing years. The Psalmist wrote, "They (the righteous) will still bear fruit in old age; they will stay fresh and green. . ." (Psalm 92:14-15) Later, in a list of those who should praise the Lord, he included "young men and maidens, old men and children". (Psalm 148:12)

The prophet Isaiah promised to all ages, ". . . those who hope in the Lord will renew their strength. They will soar on wings like eagles; they will run and not grow weary, they will walk and not faint."(Isaiah 40:31) True, that promise contains some poetic hyperbole; physically, we do become weary. But the truth stands: when our strength wanes, He gives restoration; when we must go through the "valley of the shadow of death", He is with us, renewing our hope. There are no dead ends on life's pathway when you're walking with God!

Seasons of Life

Spring, summer, fall, winter – that's the natural progression of the year. And there are seasons of life. Children become youth, then young adults, then mature adults, and, finally, senior adults. The pressures are different at each stage. From youth's raging hormones to adult responsibilities to the physical and mental deterioration of the elderly – the aging process requires major adjustments.

God is needed as the center-point to hold us steady and smooth the transitions. He doesn't fail us – whether we're young, old, or somewhere between! The Psalmist testified, "Since my youth, O God, You have taught me. , ." (Psalm 71:17) Isaiah recorded God's promise to the elderly: "Even to your old age and gray hairs I am He; I am He who will sustain you. . ." (Isaiah 46:4) We don't have to become cranky or self-centered or stubborn. Late in life, the old-time evangelist Bud Robinson developed diabetes. When he asked his doctor to explain the disease, he was told he simply had too much sugar in his blood. He responded, "Well, I declare! I've always prayed God would make me a sweet old man, and now He's overdone it!"

Scientists tell us we begin to die the moment we are born. Body cells die all the time and are replaced by new ones. If we stop growing, we die. That's a physical fact. But it's also a fact that our spirits are immortal. God designed us to live forever. This physical life is preparation for eternal life. Eternity awaits us. And He wants us to spend it with Him. Even if the calendar says life is almost over, God says it's just beginning. Jesus didn't die on the cross just to give us abundant life here; most of all, it was to give us eternal life in heaven. In Christ, our spirits bathe in the fountain of eternal youth.

That's God's plan for ageless aging.

Life With a Purpose

Millions have read and studied Rick Warren's book, <u>The Purpose Driven Life.</u> Frank Moore's book, <u>The Power to be Free,</u> focuses on the quest for the Spirit-filled life. These books are right on target. A worth-while purpose for living is vital. And it's essential to keep us from "dying on the vine" as we age. "What is my purpose for living?" is a question all of us need to answer. Otherwise, we are like sheep in the wilderness nibbling at the nearest blade of grass, then going aimlessly to the next until we've lost any sense of direction. There are so many "blades of grass" in our world. The variety changes with age, but the allurement is always present.

Personal interests, desires, and ambitions are not necessarily wrong, but as the Apostle Paul wrote, we need to "take captive every thought to make it obedient to Christ." (II Corinthians 10:5) That's living a purpose-driven life; a life centered in doing God's will, in bringing glory to our Lord, in using our abilities to leave a positive imprint on the world.

Where do you start, in finding your life purpose? Obviously, you begin with God's plan for you. Ask Him to reveal it to you. Then, take an honest look at yourself. Assess your strengths and weaknesses. How do you see yourself? Can you look beyond your faults and failures? Do you accept yourself as God created you?

Someone has described this as "being comfortable in your own skin". Your skin may be wrinkling, your age spots spreading, but your spirit can be smooth and clear.

Keep Growing

The majestic Sequoia tree, when struck and damaged by lightning, grows a new top. Life brings storms. Sometimes your spirit suffers injury. But you can be like the tree; keep reaching upward and growing – even if you have to "grow a new top". Actor Maurice Chevalier once commented: "Age is bothersome only when you stop to coddle it." Keep growing in your spirit and you won't have that problem. Don't let it harden and shrivel; keep it soft and mellow. Here's a good adage: "Blessed are the flexible, for they shall bend, not break." Just as the wings of an airplane must be able to flex, so must your "wings" adjust to life's changes.

The prophet Joel implied there's a difference between the dreams and visions of the young and the old, when he prophesied, ". . . your old men will dream dreams and your young men will see visions." (Joel 2:28) But that distinction is not compulsory. There's no age limit on visionary dreams. There can be fresh dreams and challenging goals at any age. And it's necessary for continued personal growth.

A good attitude toward life seems to come naturally to some. But most of us have to work at it. Following the 1997

death of Brandon Tartikoff, former president of NBC, someone
commented, "Life didn't always smile on him, but he always smiled
on life." What a beautiful epitaph! But, more than that, it represents
a determination to triumph over circumstances, rather than living
under them.

Norman Vincent Peale influenced millions with his teaching
of "the power of positive thinking". The opposite of that is negative
thinking. And that's bad, whatever one's age. We have a choice.
One attitude promotes personal growth, while the other generates
deterioration.

We tend to grow as we expand our horizons. We need to
build bridges, not fences or walls. One of life's great tragedies is a
hermit-like existence that isolates one into a catacomb of loneliness.
Someone has wisely observed we need some old friends to help us
grow old and many new friends to help us stay young. That requires
taking the friendship initiative, else old friendships will die and new
ones will never be born. To have friends requires being a friend. One
of the blessings of true friendship is that it helps keep us from being
too focused on ourselves.

When D. L. Moody was approaching the end of his life,
someone asked permission to write his biography. He refused, saying
"a man's life story should never be written while he is still living".
What is important is how it ends, not how it began. The way we deal

with life at every age will write our story. Every period is important. But Moody was right. The story is not complete until that final chapter is written.

Applying the Principle – Discussion Questions

1. Why do some people age prematurely?

2. What are characteristics of a person who is "aging gracefully"?

3. Why do so many adults want to appear younger than their chronological age?

4. Does Western culture overemphasize youth, to the neglect of the aged?

5. How can we break down "generation barriers"?

6. Does ones' life purpose change with age?

7. What does it mean to "expand your horizons"?

CHAPTER 12

BELIEVING IS SEEING

It's all so confusing! Do we believe because we see, or do we see because we believe? The conventional wisdom is that "seeing is believing". But our principle disagrees. So, who's right?

Dr. Robert Schuller has described the difference between an optimist and a pessimist. The pessimist says, "I'll believe it when I see it." The optimist says, "I'll see it when I believe it." According to Dr. Schuller, you're an optimist if you agree with our principle. If, on the other hand, you're one who wants to see it before you'll believe it, perhaps you need some new insight.

Actually, believing and seeing are not polar opposites, nor are they mutually exclusive. Rather, they are parallel senses, each complementing the other. It's not like the proverbial question, "Which comes first: the chicken or the egg?" It has more in common with the Apostle James' discussion of the faith versus deeds issue. In James 2:14-18, he wrote: "What good is it, my brothers, if a man claims to have faith but has no deeds? Can such faith save him? . . . But someone will say, 'You have faith, I have deeds'. Show me your faith without deeds, and I will show you my faith by what I do."

Likewise, both believing and seeing are important. They are partners in our life experience. But I would suggest believing is the senior partner.

The Faith Factor

Consider how many things in your life would not happen without a faith that precedes the event. It's 6:00 a.m., and the annoying ring of your alarm clock ends your night of sleep. And why does it ring? Because, the night before, you set it to awaken you. And why did you do that? Because you believed it would. Now you find the off button and stop that obnoxious noise. Barely awake, you climb out of bed, stagger to the bathroom, and flip a light switch. Why? Because you believe the light will come on. And it does. You open the shower door and turn on the faucet. Why? Because you believe a refreshing spray of water will come. And so it continues throughout the day. Because you believe, you act. And, as a result, you see.

"Faith" is just a small word – but a powerful one. It is:

The eye that sees the invisible,

The ear that hears the inaudible,

The hand that touches the intangible,

The tongue that tastes heaven's manna,

The nose that detects the aroma of the supernatural.

Faith is the ultimate sixth sense. It takes the human senses to a deeper level. It's not limited by time, space, bank accounts, or seemingly impossible circumstances.

Faith is hope taken to a higher level. Hebrews 11:1 makes this clear: "Now faith is being sure of what we hope for and certain of what we do not see." It has the addition of the confidence factor. This is not to disparage hope; it's vital for victorious living. In fact, the Apostle Paul listed it as one of the "big three" (faith, hope, and love). But, without confidence, it falls short. Confidence needs continual nurture and renewal. And it needs direction – the direction of the Holy Spirit. Otherwise, it degenerates into mere self-confidence.

Many of Jesus' statements about faith are recorded in the Gospels. One of the most challenging occurred when two blind men begged Him to heal them. (Matthew 9:27-31) After touching their eyes, He told them, "according to your faith will it be done to you." That's a requirement for all of us, not just those blind men.

Most of us are not "giants of faith". Sometimes we have to pray the prayer of the father who confessed to Jesus: "I do believe; help me overcome my unbelief!" (Mark 9:24) D. L. Moody once said there are three kinds of faith: *struggling faith* – like a man in deep water swimming desperately; *clinging faith* – like an exhausted swimmer clutching the side of a boat; *resting faith* – like a person safely inside the boat and able to reach out to help someone else. The good news: faith can grow to a higher level!

Reality Check

If believing is the "senior partner", what is the role of seeing? It's a reality check for believing – much like deeds constitute the "proof in the pudding" for faith. Otherwise, desires or emotions may lead us astray. And what is "seen" needs to be compatible with both Scripture and common sense.

A recent newspaper article on "Faith", which originated in the Los Angeles Times, related some strange "miracles", in which religious figures mysteriously appeared in unusual places. Examples it cited included: a worker in a California candy factory who saw, in the glob of candy at the mixing vat's spout, an amazing likeness of the Virgin Mary standing in prayer. In another instance, a woman making burritos saw the face of Jesus in the pattern of skillet burns on a tortilla. She built a shrine to house the Jesus tortilla, which was blessed by a priest. Thousands came to see it. Another example of questionable faith was the "miracle nun bun" – a cinnamon bun which was said to have the likeness of Mother Teresa. Such incidents occur frequently, and the response of dubious faith detracts from the validity of genuine faith.

In Matthew 17:20, Jesus made a strange statement: ". . . if you have faith as small as a mustard seed, you can say to this mountain, 'move from here to there' and it will move." That's pretty impressive! But remember this: Jesus was not an advocate of frivolous faith. He wouldn't approve of you waking up some morning and deciding, "I'm gonna move me a mountain today." Why? "Well, just because I can. Besides, it would impress my friends." Obviously, Jesus wasn't speaking of literal mountains. But there are lots of "mountains" in your life you might like to move. You have the equipment to do it. Jesus called it faith. It is powerful.

There's a joke about a woodpecker that was hammering away on a tree trunk when a lightning bolt struck the tree and destroyed it. As the bird flew away, he exclaimed, "I didn't know I had so much power in my beak!" We, too, are equipped with more power than we realize. But we need to be sure that, when we use our faith on serious life issues, we do it with a deep sense of awe and reverence.

Faith needs to rest on a solid foundation and be used for a worthwhile purpose. In a <u>Reflecting God </u>devotional, Garry D. Pate wrote, "When faith stands on the promise of God, it isn't presumption." Psalm 37:4 says "Delight yourself in the Lord and He will give you the desires of your heart." That's more than a spirit-lifting promise; it's a formula for believing that results in seeing. Our desires must be God-centered, not self-centered. Our will needs to be aligned with His will for the formula to work.

It's a fact of life that faith doesn't always bring the anticipated result. One day a duck hunter was bragging to his hunting buddies about his shooting skills. Just then, a duck flew over. He took aim and fired. The bird flew on. Turning to his friends, he said, with an awed voice, "You are now witnessing a miracle. There flies a dead duck!"

How do you react when your faith seems to have failed? Do you still believe in a miracle-working God? Can you still trust that He is "working for your good in all things?" (See Romans 8:28 NIV) If the foundation is sound and the purpose is correct, you can. The apparent failure of believing may bring a new perspective on seeing. And a fresh acceptance of God's will prevents the disillusionment of your faith.

Believing in God

The King James version of Psalm 27:13 speaks of the urgency of confidence in God: "I had fainted, unless I had believed to see the goodness of God. . ." A little girl expressed a similar truth with childlike frankness when she prayed: "Dear God, please take care of yourself or we are all sunk." For her, God was a real Person, not a theological abstraction. He was the source of her hope and the object of her faith.

"God give to us the simple faith

That little children find ---

The faith to hope, the faith to see

That clouds are silver-lined.

Give us the faith to dream bright dreams

Upon the darkest day;

And, most of all, give us the faith

To clasp our hands and pray."

--Margaret E. Sangster

Life is more complex for adults. Believing in God isn't quite as simple as for a child. But the foundation is the same. It's based upon a personal relationship – with the God who created us to have fellowship with Him. And that generates a faith that sees the hand of God in life's providence. An atheist gave as his reason for not believing in the existence of God, the fact that once he was lost in the desert, and he prayed. But God didn't answer his urgent prayer. His friend replied, "Well, something must have happened; you're here now." The atheist responded, "Yeah, I was just lucky. A crazy old prospector came along and saved me."

We shake our heads over the atheist's unwillingness to believe God answered his prayer – through the prospector. But we need to remind ourselves it's not enough to believe in God; we must continue believing in Him. In His goodness, justice, faithfulness, grace, love. When life just isn't fair. When it seems God has forgotten us. That's when we need our faith encouraged by the promises in the written Word; by remembering God's blessings of the past; by spending time in His Presence. In His good time He will prove the validity of the "believing is seeing" principle. In the words of Hebrews 11:6, ". . . He rewards those who earnestly seek Him."

Faith makes things possible, but not easy. Sometimes it's like a roll of film; it requires darkness to develop. In such times, even those who are strong in faith must practice it as a choice. When it's not easy to believe God, we must choose to believe Him. Charles Spurgeon gave a perceptive illustration. He described a fire in a house with a child trapped in a room on the third floor. A large, strong man stands on the ground under the window where the terrified child cries for help. He calls, "Jump! Drop into my arms!" Spurgeon would continue, "It is a part of faith to know that the man is there; still another part to believe him to be strong. But the essence of faith lies in trusting him enough to drop into his arms." So, in such stressful times, faith is a decision.

Believing in Yourself

It has been said that, if you don't believe in yourself, no one else will. While that might be a bit of an exaggeration, it does point out the importance of believing in yourself. It's not an issue of mere human self-confidence. It's not a personality trait; not macho manhood or feminine mystique. Rather, this assurance is based on a spiritual foundation:

Knowing *who* you are – a child of God. . . created in His

image. . . a temple of the Holy Spirit;

Knowing *what you are worth* – more than the whole world. . . enough for Jesus to die for. . . enough for the Holy Spirit to convict of guilt, then cleanse your heart.;

Knowing *where* your priorities lie – to grow in Christ-likeness. . . to serve more than to be served. . . to spend eternity in heaven.

Believing in ourselves must go beyond the who, what, and where of the present. A Sunday school teacher asked a small boy, "Who made you?" Expecting him to reply, "God", he was surprised by the answer: "Mister, I ain't done yet!" Childlike, but profound. An insight we all need. A faith that in the future we'll be better and more complete than we are today. A faith that our Creator will continue creating new things in our lives. As the boundaries of our belief are stretched, through His grace we see growth.

Believing in People

The church of which I'm a member recently completed a major building program. The theme was "It's About People". We're reminded that the purpose of all we do is for ministry to people. All kinds of people. Those who are like us and those who are different. Some are easy to believe in, while others are a challenge to faith.

There are two extremes we need to avoid. One mistake is believing in the inherent goodness of everyone. The other error is believing some are beyond redemption. We know, from Scripture, that everyone is born with a depraved nature. All have sinned. (Romans 3:23) Even those who appear to be good need salvation. On the other hand, God has transformed the lives of many who appeared to be hopelessly lost. We're not responsible for judging anyone's spiritual potential. We must leave that to God. He knows whether or not their hardened hearts can be softened. Our role is to believe everyone can be redeemed and to do all we can to reach them. So, believing in people is basic to evangelism.

There's another reason for believing in people: their human potential. Most have not reached it. A teenager brought home a school report card that reflected less than stellar performance. One teacher had commented: "He's an under-achiever." When reprimanded by his parents, the boy protested: "That's not the problem. My teacher is an over-expecter."

While expectations sometimes are unreal, most of us are, in fact, "under-achievers". Every person needs someone to believe in him or her – to help unlock the potential. And that is our opportunity to put our faith to work in the marketplace of life. Another chance to prove that "believing is seeing"!

Applying the Principle – Discussion Questions

1. What is your hardest struggle in believing before seeing?

2. What is "frivolous faith"?

3. What is the difference between faith and presumption?

4. What is the difference between "mustard seed faith" and bold faith?

5. Can a person have struggling, clinging and resting faith – all at the same time? In what way?

6. Which is most effective: a person's faith for their own needs, or faith for someone else?

7. What experience in your life has brought the greatest increase in your faith?

CHAPTER 13

WORSHIP HAPPENS IN A HEART, NOT A PLACE

That's a bold statement, coming from a "man of the cloth". Throughout my pastoral ministry, I tried to get people to worship together in one special place. On the Lord's Day. Regularly. In a building designed for worship. The "Worship Service" was the centerpiece of the church schedule. And that's customary for most congregations. I believe this is pleasing to God. And it meets deep needs in people's lives.

Consider some of the names used for the designated place of worship: *sanctuary* – that suggests a place of shelter from life's storms; *House of Worship* – signifies a place of family togetherness; *Worship Center* – implies focused worship; *auditorium* – indicates performers and spectators, all of whom need to be participants.

What qualifies as a house of worship? A beautiful building? A storefront room? A school gymnasium? A jungle "brush arbor"? A nature setting, such a mountainside or seashore? The answer: God accepts all of these. He is neither impressed by the impressive nor offended by the simple. And human spiritual needs may be met in all of these settings.

What about our worship aids? The list keeps getting longer! Religious symbols, stained glass windows, candles, music, preaching, prayer, drama, puppets, high tech sound systems, Powerpoint computer programs. Whatever happened to simple worship of our Creator! And, how does God feel about all of this? Well, Scripture indicates He approves of anything that enhances true worship; as long as the aids do not become the objects of our devotion. Sometimes the greatest worship aid is simply closing our eyes and allowing our spirits to bathe in the refreshing shower of His majestic presence.

Visit a dozen churches, and you'll experience a variety of worship styles. We have everything from ritualistic to freestyle; from exuberant to meditative. Many factors contribute to this diversity, including age, denominational emphases, education, and social customs. Probably you have a favorite type. If God has one, we don't know what it is. This much we do know: He desires worship from the heart, whatever its' form.

Our Principle is not meant to minimize the importance of the church family worshipping together. The writer of the epistle to the Hebrews (10:25) urged Christians to faithfully meet together – presumably for worship. The psalmist prayed, "I have seen You in the sanctuary and beheld your power and your glory." (Psalm 63:2) Then, he declared, "My soul yearns, even faints, for the courts of the

Lord; . . . better is one day in your courts than a thousand elsewhere."
(Psalm 84:2, 10) But the point is this: people gathered in a building
do not guarantee worship will occur.

We use the term "corporate worship". But, technically, there's
no such thing. Buildings do not worship; neither do groups. There
are only individuals worshipping God together. And it has to happen
in the heart. Just as it can't take place in an empty building, genuine
worship doesn't transpire in an empty heart. And it doesn't develop
in a self-centered heart. The experience must be God-centered.

Preparation for Worship

While worship of God should be a part of our daily lives,
we need special times when we are intensely focused on Him. And
that doesn't "just happen" because it's a scheduled event. *Preparation*
is necessary. Attitudes need to be adjusted; thoughts must be
disciplined; emotions require spiritual sensitizing.

Many years ago, Vance Havner wrote: "The average church
member today has no appetite for the Bread of Heaven on Sunday
because he has fed all week on the garlic and onions of Egypt."
That comment would be most appropriate for today! Our lives are
so cluttered with busy-ness. Too often we approach worship with
preoccupied minds and tense emotions. Even getting the family
ready for church can distract. As a result, we miss the blessing and

disappoint God.

An unknown poet has written:

Some go to church for just a walk;

Some go to stare and laugh and talk.

Some go there to meet a friend.

Some their idle time to spend.

Some for general observation;

Some for private speculation.

Some to sit and doze and nod –

But we should go to worship God!

In Revelation 1:10, the Apostle John wrote, "On the Lord's Day I was in the Spirit." Then follows his amazing description of Jesus in His glorified splendor and the revelation of things to come in human history. John was not just "filled with the Spirit" on the Day of Pentecost; he also was "in the Spirit" on his day of worship. His mind and heart were prepared. He was focused on God. He had shut out other voices. He was ready to receive what the Lord had for him.

What if John had not been "in the Spirit"? Would we have the book of Revelation? And, what will we miss if we are not in such a spiritual condition that our worship is real? An empty ritual leaves the heart empty.

The Purpose of Worship

The habit of worship may fill a building with people; the sounds of worship may reverberate from the walls; the act of worship may bring good feelings. But it's not real worship unless something happens in the heart. Otherwise, it's just another entertainment venue.

The primary purpose of worship should be the cultivation of relationship, not just adoration of Deity. Not to make God feel good but to help us know Him better. Not just to know Him as the Supreme Being. Not just as the Creator of the Universe. But to know Him as the personal God who wants to reveal himself more fully to us. We can't really worship without sensing His Lordship. Our concept of God affects our relationship with Him. But the reverse is true, also. Our knowledge of Him comes through relationship.

Somewhere I read of a Christian traveler in India who heard drums beating as he passed a pagan temple. He asked his guide what was the meaning. The reply: "Oh, they are waking up the gods, for it is almost time for worship." Our God doesn't need to be awakened. He "neither slumbers nor sleeps." (Psalm121:4) Rather, we worship Him so that He may awaken us to His unchanging truth, His all-inclusive love, His redeeming grace, His transforming power.

A small boy explained why he liked to be in church when

he prayed: "It makes me feel bigger than I am." Most of us can say "amen" to that – if we truly worship. King David must have had similar feelings when he wrote, in Psalm 27:1: "The Lord . . . is the stronghold of my life – of whom shall I be afraid?" Then, in verse 4, he revealed the reason for his confidence: "One thing I ask of the Lord; this is what I seek: that I may dwell in the house of the Lord all the days of my life, to gaze upon the beauty of the Lord and to seek him in his temple." Being in the presence of the Almighty God does wonders for one's confidence!

Participation in Worship

It's 10:30 a.m. Sunday. Time for worship. You arrive prepared, "in the Spirit". You are spiritually hungry. As Saint Augustine prayed centuries ago, "Thou hast made us for Thyself, and our souls are restless until they find rest in Thee." Now what? Well, the next important step is *participation*. Whatever anyone else does, determine you'll be a participant! Worship should be purpose-driven, not habit performed.

In his book, Pocket of Pebbles, Charles Hembree tells of a cartoon showing two overweight ladies talking. One of them says, "my weight loss club is having great success. We've lost 148 pounds. However, none of it is mine, personally." Rather humorous. But if the worship experience doesn't include you, that's sad. Like many things in life, participation in worship is a decision. And your heartfelt involvement will help create an atmosphere in which God can bless the entire congregation. Including you. There is strength in numbers!

What's involved in being a worship participant? A couple arrived quite late at a service. As they slipped into a back pew, the man whispered to his wife: "Perfect timing – too late for the offering and just in time for the sermon!" It's obvious something was lacking in their participation level.

Most worship services provide opportunities for us to be something more than spectators. The offering is just one of many. Music, Scripture readings, and prayer should not be mere solo performances. The words should resound in every mind and heart, even if only one voice is audible.

Participation involves more than just doing things in a service. It's not enough to sing the right notes, speak the right words, or express the right emotions. Receptivity of the mind and heart is crucial. As he greeted his pastor at the close of a service, a man gave an interesting compliment: "Great sermon, Pastor. Everything you said applies to someone I know." I, too, have received some compliments that made me wonder if my message had been deflected to someone else.

Worship should do two things: comfort the afflicted and afflict the comfortable. Sometimes we need comfort. And frequently we need to be reproved. Sometimes, even rebuked. Someone has pointed out that, while John 8:32 declares "the truth will set us free", first it must make us miserable. Jesus promised the Holy Spirit would meet both needs. (See John 16) But that occurs only where there's *receptive participation*.

Worship in Song

Music is one of the most important parts of the worship experience. Even for those of us who are musically challenged. (I don't like "political correctness", but I have to admit that sounds better than saying "he can't carry a tune in a bucket".) The Psalmist admonished us to sing joyously (Psalm 66:1), not necessarily melodiously. You don't have to be a great singer to participate in the music of worship. Do it, even if you can only mumble the words in a monotone!

I remember a retired member of one of the congregations I served. He was our "snowbird singer". Every spring, when he and his wife returned from Florida, we knew he was back without even seeing him in the congregation. His booming voice carried above the entire crowd. He wasn't trying to attract attention. He was just singing joyously. He was involved in worship. Fortunately, he sang "on tune". He wasn't a distraction; he was a blessing. And he was being blessed.

Music is a powerful aid to worship. It lifts our spirits above the burdens and struggles of life. It releases spiritual emotions that need to be expressed. It helps focus our attention on the Holy God who has come to meet with His people. Yet music also has the potential of creating division within the congregation. Music tastes differ. Time brings change in lyrics, harmony, and tempo. What was popular in the secular world 50 years ago was vastly different from what is popular today. Church music changes, too. In many churches, the old-time hymns are out; praise choruses are in. Older people tend to desire the traditional – what they have been used to. The young want something contemporary.

How can this dilemma be resolved? Church leaders must prayerfully and lovingly seek ways both needs can be met. It might be through a blended format or by multiple services with different types of music. As individual worshippers, we need flexibility and tolerance. That's true, whether we're young or old. God-centered worship makes us less self-centered. We can worship Him, even when the music and service format are not our preference. Actually, many of us need to shed some inhibitions. A little hand clapping and hand- raising might be good for us! On the other hand, the message of sacred hymns adds depth to our worship. The contemporary isn't better just because it's new. And the old isn't sacred just because of its age.

Worship With Praise

Praise in worship is different than it used to be, but it's still a vital part of worship. Spontaneous "testimonies" used to be common; sometimes praise was expressed in "shouting", as hearts overflowed with spiritual blessings. Now we sing praise choruses to magnify our Lord. Praise teams encourage us to participate in worship through music. Hand clapping and raised hands amplify our verbal adoration. However it is expressed, praise is good. And it's Scriptural. Just remember the primary goal is not to get clap-happy, but to enjoy the Presence of the God who puts a song in the heart.

"Let everything that has breath praise the Lord." (Psalm 150:6) It should be as natural as breathing! It may come from the lungs, but it originates in the heart. According to that psalm, there are many ways of expressing it, but they are shallow without genuine worship.

Who benefits most from our praise in worship? Does God get a warm, fuzzy feeling when we praise Him? I confess, I don't know. However, I do understand we humans were created in His image. Theologians make a distinction between the "natural image of God" (rational powers of intelligence, conscience, immortality, etc.) and the "moral image of God" (spiritual qualities of God-likeness, such as ethical character and holiness). Since we have the ability to enjoy praise, I assume God does, also. Beyond that, I leave the issue with the theologians.

It is certain that praise is beneficial to the sincere worshipper. It helps us focus on our Lord. It lifts our spirits. It aids our communion with our Heavenly Father. And the Bible suggests another possible result. When Jehoshaphat, king of Judah, was going into battle against overwhelming forces, he was given this promise: "Do not be afraid or discouraged because of this vast army. For the battle is not yours, but God's. Take up your positions; stand firm and see the deliverance the Lord will give you." (II Chronicles 20:15-17) Then, in verse 22, we're told, "As they began to sing and praise, the Lord set ambushes against (their enemies). . ." Notice the connection: *as they sang and praised, God set an ambush.* Praise is powerful! It can even release God's power to help us in our times of need. Sometimes we just need to praise our way through our difficulties.

Acts 16:25-40 records another proof of the power of praise. Paul and Silas are prisoners in a Philippian jail. Chains pinch their wrists. Stocks lock their feet in place. It's midnight. They start praying and singing hymns to God. And He responds with an earthquake! Shakes the prison to its foundation. Opens its' doors. Frees the prisoners.

God responds to *our* heartfelt praise, too. Brings victory in life's battles. Breaks the shackles of imprisoned spirits. Gives assurance of His unfailing love. But there is one requirement: the praise must come from a worshipping heart.

Applying the Principle – Discussion Questions

1. What helps you worship God with all your heart?

2. What can you do to better prepare for worship?

3. What is "purpose-driven worship"?

4. What does "receptive participation" mean to you?

5. What is the greatest blessing you receive from worship?

6. How can we preserve reverence in worship while promoting informality?

7. Why is praise such an important part of worship?

ACKNOWLEDGEMENTS AND CREDITS

Unless otherwise indicated, Scripture quotations are from the New International Version

Chapter 1

    1. Quoted by George K. Bowers, in <u>God – Here and Now.</u> (Warner Press, Anderson, Indiana, 1961)

    2. Rubes cartoon, by Leigh Rubin. Used by permission of Leigh Rubin and Creators Syndicate, Inc.

    3. Blondie cartoon, by Young and LeBrun. Used by permission of King Features Syndicate, Inc.

Chapter 2

    .1. Sidney J. Harris, <u>Majority of One.</u> (Houghton Mifflin, Boston, 1957)

    2. Merritt Neilson, in <u>Reflecting God</u> devotional. (WordAction Publishing Company, Kansas City, MO.)

Chapter 3

    1. Gay Jervey, "Cheating", <u>Readers' Digest</u>, March, 2006.

    2. Bette Howland, <u>Catholic Digest</u>. (New London, Connecticut)

    3. Don Wildman, in <u>American Family Association Journal,</u> February, 1993.

4. Mia Hamm, <u>Go for the Goal.</u> (Quill, New York, N.Y. 2000)

5. Cathy Better, as printed in Reistertown, Md., <u>Community Times</u>

6. Zig Ziglar, <u>See You at the Top</u>. (Pelican Publishing Company, Gretna, La. 1975)

Chapter 4

1. Calvin and Hobbes cartoon, by Bill Watterson. Dist. By Universal Press Syndicate. Reprinted with permission. All rights reserved.

2. Zig Ziglar, <u>See You at the Top</u>. (Pelican Publishing Company, Gretna, LA 1975)

3. Louisa Fletcher Tarkington, "The Land of Beginning Again." Publisher unknown.

4. George MacDonald, as quoted by David Roper in <u>Our Daily Bread</u> devotional. (RBC Ministries, Grand Rapids, MI)

Chapter 5

1. Arthur Brooks, "Who Really Cares; The Surprising Truth about Compassionate Conservatism". Reported in <u>Christianity Today</u>, February, 2007.

2. Noah Benshea, <u>Jacob the Baker</u> series. (Ballantine Books, New York, N.Y., 1990)

Chapter 6

1. David Redding, <u>The Parables He Told</u>. (Revell, Westwood, N,J., 1962)

2. Dave Brannon, devotional in <u>Our Daily Bread</u> (RBC Ministries, Grand Rapids, MI)

Chapter 7

1. Dennis DeHaan, devotional in <u>Our Daily Bread.</u> (RBC Ministries, Grand Rapids, MI)

Chapter 8

1. The Family Circus cartoon, by Bil Keane. Used by permission of King Features Syndicate.

2. Rabbi Harold Kushner, <u>When Bad Things Happen to Good People</u> (Schocken Books, New York, N.Y. 1989)

3. Joan M. Wilson, in <u>Reflecting God</u> devotional (WordAction Publishing Co., Kansas City, MO)

4. Robert Lowery, "Nothing but the Blood" (public domain)

5. Aron Rolston, as quoted in "The Up Side", <u>Guideposts,</u> April, 2005)

Chapter 9

1. Leslie Parrott, <u>The Power of Your Attitudes</u> (Beacon Hill Press, 1967)

2. Philip Yancy, "The Unnatural Act", in <u>Christianity Today</u>,

April, 1991

Chapter 10

1. For Better or for Worse comic strip. Lynn Johnston Productions. Dist. By Universal Press Syndicate. Reprinted by permission. All rights reserved.

2. C.S. Lewis, <u>The Four Loves</u> (Harcourt Brace. New York, N.Y., 1988)

Chapter 11

1. Stanley Kauffman, in <u>The New Republic</u>, (The New Republic, Washington, D.C.)

2. Dr. Andrew Weil, in <u>AARP Magazine</u>, May – June, 2007

Chapter 12

1. Gary D. Pate, in <u>Reflecting God</u> devotional (WordAction Publishing Co., Kansas City, MO)

2. Margaret E. Sangster. Excerpted from "Prayer", as printed in Elkhart, Indiana, <u>Truth</u>

Chapter 13

1. Vance Havner, <u>The Best of Vance Havner</u> (Fleming H. Revell Company, Old Tappan, New Jersey, 1969)

2. Charles Hembree, <u>Pocket of Pebbles</u> (Baker Book House, Grand Rapids, MI, 1969)

Printed in the United States
131343LV00004B/325-399/P